Keeping the Gospel in Gospel Music

A Guide for Success and Survival
in Contemporary Christian Music

By
Scott Wesley Brown

ACW Press
5501 N. 7th Ave. #502
Phoenix, AZ 85013

Publisher's Cataloging-in-Publication
(Provided by Quality Books, Inc.)

Brown, Scott Wesley
    Keeping the gospel in gospel music: a guide for success and survival in contemporary Christian music / by Scott Wesley Brown — 1st ed.
      p. cm.
    Includes bibliographical references.
    ISBN 0-9656749-6-7

    1. Contemporary Christian musicians--Religious life.
    2. Contemporary Christian musicians--Vocational guidance.
    I. Title

BV4596.M87B76 1998   248.8'8'
                               QBI98-568

To Keith Green

For all the arguments I had with him,
and the fanatic we all thought he was,
he was the first one to take a stand for
keeping the Gospel in Gospel Music!

Acknowledgements

Special Thanks to Byron Spradlin, Artists in Christian Testimony; Frank Fortunato, Operation Mobilization; Colin Harbinson, Youth with a Mission; Darrow Miller, Food for the Hungry; Gerrit Gustafson, The Worship Group; Steve Fry Ministries and Dr. John Piper, Desiring God Ministries; John Schlitt; Mike Card; Darrell Harris; John Fischer; and Steven Isaac, *Plugged In* Magazine (Focus on the Family), for so much of their powerful insight into much of the material I have presented. Thank you to Byron, Frank, Gerrit and Steve for reviewing this material and helping me craft it as accurately as possible. To Connie Morkel for going the extra mile in typing this manuscript. And, as always, to my parents Len and Dorothy Brown, and my wife Belinda along with Jessica and Hannah who have patiently stood by my side even when were thousands of miles apart!

Contents

About the Author

The past two decades have seen Scott Wesley Brown's songs recorded by Sandi Patty, Amy Grant, Bruce Carroll, Pat Boone, The Imperials, Petra, and international opera star Placido Domingo. His music has inspired musicians to reach for a higher level of excellence while moving audiences to a deeper understanding of the call to love that crystallized Scott Wesley Brown's commitment to speading the Gospel to over thirty-nine countries worldwide.

Brown's journal records covert missions behind the Iron Curtain and the first publicly promoted Christian music event in the U.S.S.R. It was during this August 1989 concert that over 15,000 Soviets heard the passionate cry for love and compassion while the Spirit moved some 2,000 to join in the family of Christ. Scott Wesley Brown stood side-by-side with East German brothers and sisters as the Berlin wall came down, marking another victory for the Kingdom. He has taken over 100 musicians to trips to the mission field and provided hundreds of musical instruments to musicians and mission-aries in third world and restricted access countries.

While Scott Wesley Brown understands the global mission, he also understands family. His wife Belinda and two daughters, Jessica and Hannah live in Franklin, Tennessee and are involved in the home school movement.

Scott is also a featured singer at Promise Keepers, and has written several songs for these events including the theme song "Godly Men."

He has recorded over twenty albums and recently was the first American Christian artist to record an entire album in Africa using the unique sounds and rythms of the African peoples.

Foreword

"*Gospel Music*—what an oxymoron; a phrase that doesn't always make sense."

I don't want to feel that way about gospel music but sometimes I do. And do you know why? Just review for a minute.

The GOSPEL...according to the Bible, is the good news that there is the true and living holy God-over-all. And though every one of us has violated His holy law through our chronic bent towards self-rule in defiance of His supremacy—and have hell to pay for it—He has shown His amazing love and compassion for us all by providing His Son Jesus as payment for the penalty of eternal separation from Him we ought pay. All we have to do is confess we're lawbreakers in heart and deed, and cry out to Him in sorrow and faith for His forgiveness. He promises to forgive us, bring us spiritual life through His own Holy Spirit, and lavish us with every spiritual blessing (including His access, care and unfathomable resources for life and living). Where once we were lost, now we're found; we were blind but now can see. That's really good news.

MUSIC...in the context of human life and experience...is that God-created mysterious medium through which...and where in...there often seems to exist the joining, and the releasing, of a mystical intersection of divine and human creativity. An intersection sometimes so intimate that our souls lay bare before us. An intersection sometimes so powerful that our 'groanings too deep for words' well up into expression. An intersection sometimes so awesome that our hearts seem touched by God Himself. Music is a medium able to weave almost seamlessly into the other marvels of human media and relationships—story telling, poetry, movement, painting, design, rituals, ceremony, pageantry; and on and on. Music, one of those marvels of creativity that assures us we are humans and not just animals: creatures with spirits; who can be made alive when touched (not by an angel) but by the Spirit of Jesus Himself. Music, one of those marvelous experience-places wherein we can actually marinate in the majesty and glory of God-with-us. For me that is music to my ears.

Scott Wesley Brown is one of the few in the last twenty-five years who has taken the "moron" out of the oxymoron of Gospel Music.

Scott has actually put the two ingredients Gospel and Music together in ways that have clearly glorified the most high God and His Son, Jesus the Messiah. And, from my vantage point, Scott has done so at great expense to his career...for the sake of getting on with the business of the God's Kingdom.

So, who better to bring a clarion call to put the Gospel back into Gospel Music—a call to Christians in the contemporary Christian music business, Christians in the arts, and in general Christians worldwide?

Gospel Music is not really about career, fame, or fortune...though some have tried to make it that way. So as you read this book keep your antenna up expecting God to more clearly define for you things like ministry, purpose of music in God's economy of things, and heart focus of the person who possesses musical or artistic endowments. Scott Wesley Brown not only shares information he's learned, he shares the heart God has developed in him: a heart for worship, a heart for obedience (no matter what the cost to career or to personal agendas), a heart for God's world mission of declaring His glory and His preeminence and His salvation to all peoples.

Get ready for a read that may shake, even reshape, the very way you define gospel music. I'm praying you'll not be the same when you're done. I pray you will be more focused, and even more radical for the glory of God—which is the work of the Gospel of Christ.

And when you've finished this book I pray you'll better be able to say with the Apostle Paul, that you are...

"A servant of Christ Jesus, called to be (a special messenger) and set apart for the gospel of God—the gospel he promised beforehand through his prophets in the Holy Scriptures regarding his Son...Jesus Christ our Lord....I am not ashamed of the gospel, because it is the power of God for the salvation of everyone who believes: first for the Jew, then for the Gentile" Romans 1: 1-4; 16.

Rev. Byron Spradlin
President, Artists in Christian Testimony
Nashville, TN
February, 1998

"Faithful are the wounds of a friend,
but deceitful are the kisses of an enemy."
Proverbs 27:6 NASB

INTRODUCTION

A powerful tool must be used in a proper way. In the hands of the master chef, a gas flame is used to prepare a feast. In the hands of the ignorant, the same flame can be dangerous. Controlled by the arsonist, the flame becomes deadly. Likewise with contemporary Christian music: if biblical principles are violated, using this tool can be meaningless, divisive, or destructive, even when the music is used with the best intentions.
  - Steve Miller, *The CCM Debate*

Long ago when early American frontiersmen were forging the path to the west and claiming rugged land for new settlements, building towns, homes and churches, an Indian made a provoking observation. A cowboy asked the Indian what his impression was of the Bible-thumping preacher whose voice echoed throughout the canyons every Sunday morning. The Indian folded his arms and said "Loud thunder, flashing lightning, big wind...no rain!"

This is a book about rain and how our music and ministries can produce life-giving rain in the midst of all the loud thunder, flashy lightning and big wind of the contemporary Christian music industry. If there is no rain then we are just like the Bible-thumping preacher of old. We will blaze across the frontier of Christian music leaving behind a legacy of powerful display with pitiful results.

The book of Jude gives a stern warning about men who are like clouds with no rain. They are described as those who rush after profit and shepherds who feed only themselves, wild waves and wandering stars in the blackest darkness.

But the Bible also gives us a contrast and describes the heart that longs to minister and produce in others a harvest of righteousness.

> "Let my teaching fall like rain and
> my words descend like dew,
> like showers on new grass,
> like abundant rain on tender plants.
> I will proclaim the name of the Lord,
> Oh praise the greatness of our God."
> (Deuteronomy 32:2, 3)

This is a book for all those whose hearts have been stirred by God to be rainmakers in the ministry of contemporary Christian music whether in the industry or not. It is for aspiring young artists as much as it is for seasoned professionals.

It is not a book giving tips on how to make it in the music business. It is a lot of deep digging into God's word and examining the lives and stories of artists, musicians and priests who, like you and me, struggled in the battlefield of self worth, self pleasure, self accomplishment, and their relationship with the God who created them for His glory and their own true fulfillment.

U.S. President Teddy Roosevelt once said, "A leader understands that failure is the backdoor to success." If we can learn from the failures of these biblical figures, and from our own failures, then perhaps we can find the "backdoor" to true success in both the world and the kingdom.

Roosevelt also said, "A leader invariably lives his life as a sincere imitator of the best attributes of others. Heroes always have heroes." So we will also examine the lives of biblical heroes and pray that God will give us the grace to reflect the attributes He instilled in these men which made them heroes. We need real heroes today in contemporary Christian music if we are to leave any lasting legacy.

I wish I could claim credit for all the powerful insights presented, but I must give credit where it is due. Having been involved in Christian music since 1973 I have collected many notebooks filled with the teachings and sayings of so many wise men and women of God. Their insight into God's truths and character have helped shape my destiny, not only as an artist but as a sojourner in the Christian journey.

Yours for keeping the Gospel in Gospel Music,

Scott Wesley Brown

Chapter One
Twentieth Century Babel

Remember, the road to Jerusalem is also the road away from Jerusalem.
 - C.S. Lewis

It must have been well over 100 degrees in the scorching hot sun. The tar pits scattered across the low marshy terrain emitted a hideous smoke which burned in the eyes of the brick layers. Sweat trickled down their faces as they proudly gazed at the tower which rose defiantly toward the sky. "More bricks" the foreman yelled as the hot tar oozed from between the freshly laid bricks.

The workers scurried about like ants as they carried loads of the thoroughly baked bricks up the crude scaffolds. Others dipped their hand carved ladles into the steamy tar pits that lay outside the city walls. An eerie excitement filled the air. Somehow destiny seemed to smile upon this disenfranchised people who had migrated east in search of a new homeland.

For generations the stories had been passed down. The mountain paradise that once belonged to their great father had long been lost, forfeited because of the wrath of the unknown God. The flood waters had receded, sweeping away the bones of their ancestors to the four corners of the earth. But this was the day of a new dawn. These were the ones who would survive, those who would stand against the fury and the wrath. Nothing would be impossible for them as the tower climbed brick by brick towards the heavens. Although it went unspoken, everyone knew they could rival God himself. And Nimrod contemptuously folded his arms in proud confidence as he gazed upon the city we would know as Babel.

Come Let Us Build

It may seem strange to begin a book on Gospel music (Contemporary Christian Music - CCM) going back several thousand years to the Mesopotamian plain of Shinar. But I am convinced that a good glimpse at the tower of Babel holds great insight into the disillusionment, frustration, and drivenness Christian musicians face as they struggle to build a career in the music industry.

The Christian artist is caught in the balancing act between business and ministry. Often one side shines at the expense of the other.

With the secular industry as the only model of how the business operates, the Christian artist often succumbs to worldly schemes to advance his career. Some of these make good healthy business sense, while others may be antithetical to the very Gospel he proclaims.

Yet an even greater danger lies in how the worldly obsession of "making it big" often clouds the original vision and calling of the Christian artist. This then drives a ministry that set out to make a name for Jesus instead of itself.

This obsession goes further than the good ol' American dream and work ethic. Today's "pop icon" worshiping world, ala *Entertainment Tonight* and *People* magazine, has created an insatiable appetite for all the perks of stardom.

The fabric of true heroes has been replaced by polyester poets. Even Jay Leno has fun with his street interviews where the average guy knows more about George of the Jungle than he does about George Washington.

The non-Christian world makes no excuse that sex sells. Yet in the Christian music world, "sex appeal" has become a major consideration in the signing of artists.

Words like "marketability" have replaced "responsibility" and "accountability." We measure success by "units sold" rather than "hearts told" and the focus is on "performing" rather than "transforming!"

Thousands of aspiring Christian artists flock to Christian music conferences to find that secret key to building a career in Christian music.

> *Words like "marketability" have replaced "responsibility" and "accountability."*

And that brings us back to our story about Babel. What was so wrong with building a city? After all, man needed a place to work, live, and raise his children. And what was so wrong about a tower? If God is against tall buildings then what about our modern day sky scrapers? Surely height wasn't the issue? Could it have been the new technology of using bricks instead of stone and tar instead of mortar which angered God?

To understand Babel we need to go back further. First consider the backdrop. The Babel event follows the "Fall" and the "Flood." Before the Fall man forfeited God's fellowship and the perfect paradise of Eden to exert his own selfhood. He chose what he deemed "good for food," pleasing to the eye," and "desirable for gaining wisdom." Adam ate from the forbidden tree described as the tree of the knowledge of good and evil (Genesis 4:6) even though God had set him in perfect paradise, giving him dominion over all the earth.

God promised Adam security, posterity, and fulfillment in all things if he would only demonstrate obedience, by specifically not eating from that one tree.

J.I. Packer states that the issue was whether Adam would let God tell him what was good and bad for him or would he seek to decide that for himself, in disregard of what God had said. By eating from this tree Adam would, in effect, be claiming that he could know and decide what was good and evil for him without any reference to God. By eating the forbidden fruit the result was an anti-God, self-aggrandizing mindset.[1]

This is the mindset we have inherited along with hearts that endlessly long to be satisfied and fulfilled with all that God originally intended for us in the garden.

John Milton's book *Paradise Lost* captures the sentiment of the great depths of what was forfeited in the garden. God in effect was saying, "I will satisfy you, I will fulfill you, I will protect you, I will provide for you, I will love you and keep you." Adam essentially said, "But I know better."

John Piper, in his book *Future Grace*, states that "**God is most glorified in us when we are most satisfied in him.**"[2] But this deep satisfaction was lost in the garden and ever since Man has turned to himself to "scratch the insatiable itch of self-fulfillment" as C.S. Lewis puts it.[3] But we were never meant to fulfill ourselves. Piper explains "We are but images of God, not the real thing."[4] Only God can fulfill us.

Genesis chapters three through eleven describes the devastating results of the fall and man's misdirected search to find true pleasure and fulfillment in life.

"The Lord saw how great man's wickedness on earth had become, and that every inclination of the thoughts of his heart was only evil all the time. The Lord was grieved that he had made man on the earth, and his heart was filled with pain. So the Lord said "I will wipe mankind, whom I have created, from the face of the earth - men and animals, and creatures that move along the ground, and birds of the air-for I am grieved that I have made them. But Noah found favor in the eyes of the Lord." (Genesis 6:5-8)

John Piper describes the result of man's pride and wickedness:

"Sin is what you do when your heart is not satisfied with God. No one sins out of duty. We sin because it holds out some promise of happiness. That promise enslaves us until we believe that God is more to be desired that life itself (Psalm 63:3) which means that the power of sin's promise is broken by the power of God's. All that God promises to be for us in Jesus stands over against what sin promises to be for us without Him."[5]

Adam yielded to the temptation that befell the devil himself. "For God knows that when you eat of it your eyes will be opened, AND YOU WILL BE LIKE GOD..." the serpent craftily said. (Genesis 3:5)

Satan used on Adam and Eve the very pernicious logic demonstrated in his own heavenly fall. His message, 'YOU WILL BE LIKE GOD!' is still his message today, especially in the arena of our current pop-culture. It permeates the music industry! As heaven's fallen musician and worship leader (Ezekiel 28:13; Isaiah 14:11) Satan's same nefarious but subtle scheme to steal God's glory is the driving force behind many musicians today.

"I will exalt my throne above the stars of God; I will also sit on the   mount (God's holy mountain) of the congregation on the farthest sides of the north; I will ascend the heights of the clouds *I will be like the Most High*." (Isaiah 14:13-14, emphasis added)

Consider the late rock musician Frank Zappa's comment "I am the devil's advocate. We have our worshipers who are called 'groupies'. Girls will give their bodies to musicians as you would give a sacrifice to a god."[6]

And then there's the story of the young Danny "Dee" Snider who said "Alice Cooper is my hero. I used to have this picture of Alice over my sink, and every morning I would bow down to it"[7] Danny went on to form the now disbanded rock group Twisted Sister whose rebellious message and stage show was hellacious!

In a television interview with Dick Clark, pop singer Madonna said her greatest ambition was to "rule the world!" Could this is be the "you shall be like God" mentality infecting Madonna, even though her comment was probably said "tongue in cheek"?

Shrines have been erected to many pop-stars. At the Church of Elvis, fans meet to receive a touch of his presence. There is even a church centered around the late Kurt Cobain of Nirvana, where instead of singing hymns, they sing the maligned songs of Nirvana. And the first International Church of Tori Amos meets via the Internet on a page called "The Altar Room" where devoted fans are invited to share testimonies of how Tori has changed their life.[8]

And so the Fall led to the Flood, and even after the Flood, humankind continued to demonstrate rebellion. God's explicit command to Noah and his sons to multiply and spread out through all the earth (Genesis 9:7) was ignored. Well, maybe they got the multiply part down, but they were completely disobedient to the command to scatter throughout the earth. God had a reason for this and eventually He forced them to scatter. Let's look at the story.

> "Now the whole world had one language and a common speech. As men moved eastward, they found a plain in Shinar and settled there. They said to each other, 'Come, let's make bricks and bake them thoroughly." They used brick instead of stone, and tar for mortar. Then they said, "Come let us build ourselves a city, with a tower that reaches to the heavens, so that we may make a name for ourselves and not be scattered over the face of the whole earth" (Gen. 11:1-4).

There are several points to be made here:

1. At this point in history there are no nations, (ethnic divisions) only one common people with one common language.
2. They moved eastward to a plain in Shinar
3. They were building a city with a tower they hoped would reach to the heavens.
4. They wanted to make a name for themselves
5. They did not want to be scattered over the face of the whole earth.

The following may be somewhat speculative, but I believe the points are worthy of our discussion especially as they apply to issues in our lives and ministries.

1. *One common people with a common language.*

What they shared in common was not only a language of speech, but also a language of the heart; a language of pride. Notice the self-centeredness. "Come let **us** build **ourselves** a city with a tower that reaches to the heavens, so that **we** may make a name for **ourselves**." Self determination, self exaltation!

2. *They moved eastward to a plain in Shinar.*

Both Ezekiel's vision of God's Temple and the disciple John's revelation of the New Jerusalem make many symbolic references to Eden, set high on a mountain with rivers issuing from the lush plenitude of this garden paradise.

Yet after the Fall and the Flood, the sons of Cush migrated eastward to the low marshy lands of Mesopotamia with its unrelenting winds and fetid hot tar pits. It wasn't exactly prime real estate! It was literally "the pits!"

3. *They built a city with a tower they hoped would reach the heavens.*

According to the *Geneva Study Bible*, Nimrod, whose name literally means **"we shall rebel,"** is identified later in Jewish tradition as the builder of the Tower. The Tower marks the beginning of man's post-flood quest for domination and autonomy over God in an attempt to find significance in his own achievements.

If the high experience of Eden was lost, why not recreate it by building a tower that would reach to the heavens? Pride built the tower and once again Satan's delusive motive **"You shall be like God"** raised it's ugly head.

I should add, parenthetically, that in building the city "they used brick instead of stone, and tar instead of mortar" (Genesis 11:3) Was this possibly even a further sign of their unbelief or distrust in God? Perhaps they remembered the Flood and, just for extra security, built a city using materials that were more water-resistant. They insisted on baking the brick thoroughly and using the local tar to assemble it all together. Perhaps more than water-resistant, the objective was God-resistant!

4. They wanted to make a name for themselves.

Was this not an attempt to achieve immortality? "Name" connotes fame and progeny. "A good name is more desirable than great riches," says Proverbs 22:1. But this wasn't what Nimrod had in mind. The kind of name he and the people desired was simply a sick, ego-driven desire to bring glory to themselves!

5. They did not want to be scattered over the face of the whole earth.

God explicitly commanded Noah and his sons to increase upon the earth (Genesis 9:7). Why was God concerned with man scattering? The Lord knew man's prideful and arrogant heart was encouraged all the more as man rallied together in one region and spoke a common language. The sin of pride grew like a bacteria in a jar and the Lord saw that "nothing they plan to do will be impossible for them" (Genesis 11:6) including self-destruction - ultimately.

John Piper says "Pride is turning away from God specifically to take satisfaction in self. Pride lies at the root of every turning from God. It is the root of every act of distrust toward God."[9] God opposes the proud (James 4:6), and it is clear in this event that God not only opposed this proud people but sovereignly acted in a swift and decisive move to break down that pride. When God confused their language and caused them to scatter abroad it was not so much an act of judgment, but actually both an " act of mercy" and a "divide and conquer strategy."

The sin of pride, like an infectious disease, was surely bringing spiritual if not even physical death to mankind. By scattering them, God was protecting and preserving them. If everyone in your house or office or school has the flu, more than likely you will catch the flu.

God calls those who belong to Him to be separate. We are a separate people. In Leviticus 15:3 He commanded the Israelites to separate themselves from things that make them unclean so they will not die. In Ezra 9:1 God rebukes His people for not being separate from the neighboring peoples with their detestable practices. This affected Ezra so much that he tore his tunic and cloak and pulled his hair from his head!

God separates to protect and preserve. In Genesis 11 He is demonstrating His love and mercy upon a rebellious, prideful people.

In the same stroke, this "divide and conquer strategy" is where God literally creates the "nations." God will now deal with each nation (clan, family, tongue) one by one. This act is expressly "missionary." Genesis 10 is called the "Table of Nations" and gives us a list of the original seventy nations.

So what does all this Biblical pontification have to do with contemporary Christian music?

Remember the verse "unless the Lord builds the house, its builders labor in vain?" (Psalm 127:1) As we have already seen, Babel was born out of the "I did it my way" syndrome. It was man conceived, man driven and man centered. And in the end, it was all a fake. It was Nimrod's counterfeit Kingdom to replace what had been lost in the garden.

- Adam forfeited God's glorious sanctuary
- Nimrod built a new one
- Adam forfeited a good name
- Nimrod would make a new one

I want to be careful not to overstate the resemblance between building the tower of Babel and building a career in Christian music. The Kingdom of darkness has tried to invade the Christian music camp, but there is still a great deal of light coming from its tents. It is always easier to curse the darkness than it is to shine the light. Therefore, I have tried not to dwell "unreasonably" in cursing the darkness. I have tried to shine more light so that the Christian artist can see his way through the labyrinth of CCM and find his true calling and fulfillment in Christ alone.

As the saying goes "Don't throw the baby out with the bath water." I agree, but we must empty the tub from time to time. This is one of those times.

A Name for Ourselves

Like the world, it is easy for Christian music to become **more artist driven than art driven**, where personality and image reign over art (and it's message) and is the driving force behind the sale of that art. The Christian musician can easily become more **market driven than ministry-led**, where he bases his value on album sales or concert attendance. He can become obsessed with "making it" or becoming the "hottest new artist making a name for himself." With our own awards programs, our own top ten playlists, our own celebrity magazines, Christian music dangles this towering temptation before him. And if he is not biblically grounded in maturity, he is likely to enter into unhealthy competition, focusing on self-adulation and false measures of success and financial greed.

For example what kind of messages are Christian magazines sending (to both the artist and the audience) when they conduct reader polls to rank Christian artists in such categories as "most photogenic," "best dressed," "Mr. or Mrs. Congeniality," or "best hairdo?" Even more baffling is the claim by one particular magazine that these are "the awards that really matter."[10]

This kind of thinking has nothing to do with the true call of Gospel music, yet some artists thrive on this kind of attention. Sadly, these magazines get caught up in the same ostentatious hype found in superficial teeny bopper magazines! Ranking artists in popularity polls debases the dignity of Christian music and creates a dangerous hierarchy among artists while feeding the audience with worldly values. We end up looking just like the world. We are a sub-culture "in" the world yet, at the same time, have become "of the world" reversing Jesus' prayer in John 17.

In his book *Roaring Lambs*, Bob Briner says, "We feel we are making a difference because we are so important to ourselves. We have created a phenomenal subculture with our own media, entertainment, educational system, and political hierarchy that we have the sense that we're doing a lot. But what we've really done is create a ghetto that is easily dismissed by the rest of society"[11]

One reason we give attention to such trivial things as "best hairdo" is because Christians are caught up in the same star-studded delusion of America's obsession with the beautiful and the glamorous! The Christian musician is not excluded from this deception.

Some Christian companies will try to tell you they are just trying to "image" their artists. My question is whose image are they shooting for? Is it Hollywood or Heaven? I know several mature Christian artists who are tremendously talented, anointed, full of wisdom, and experienced, who can't get any attention from a Christian record company because they don't have "the right look." This "image" issue was so stirringly addressed in the November '96 issue of *CCM* magazine. The article was on Bob Bennett, one of Christian music's most creative and prolific songwriters and artists. Yet the very industry that boasts of his awesome talent and spiritual maturity is reluctant to embrace his music because he does not fit the "image."

In an earlier article (*CCM* May '96) Steve Ford, Executive Director of Marketing Development for STARSONG Records said, "If we weren't in a society that was visually oriented and all we were taking was raw talent and God's ability that He has given, then Bob Bennett would have been signed rather than Michael English. Bob Bennett is one of the most brilliant artists I know, but people respond as much to image as message."

I wonder how Jesus would have fared with the norms of today's Christian music scene?

> "He had no beauty or majesty to attract us to him, nothing in his appearance that we should desire him. He was despised and rejected by men, a man of sorrows and familiar with suffering. Like one from whom men hide their faces he was despised and we esteemed him not" (Isaiah 53:2-3).

I know of several artists who have experienced calloused rejection from Christian music companies because they did not have "sex appeal" as one executive admitted. But this is not the language or the logic of the Kingdom. It is the commercial rhetoric of the pop icon worshipping world. It is another example of how far Christian music can stray from ministry and kingdom values.

One of the greatest theological minds ever known is that of Saint Thomas Aquinas. His insights into classic Christian doctrine have been foundational to the church. He is ranked among such giants as Martin Luther, John Calvin, and Jonathan Edwards. Yet Thomas Aquinas was physically disproportioned. He had unusually big feet, broad shoulders, and an extremely large head for his body. In school, Thomas was the target of many practical jokes and crude comments. One day a great professor overheard a class making fun of Thomas and calling him a "dumb ox." The professor, recognizing the genius of Aquinas, turned to the class and said "Yes, but this dumb ox will change the world!"

Another obsession in Christian music today is wanting to emulate the secular award shows. When people start referring to the Dove Awards as the "Christian Grammys," should not a red flag should go up? Is not the crown of righteousness award enough? (2 Timothy 4:8). Are we like the Pharisees who need to strut their stuff for the praises of men? (John 12:43).

What a pressure cooker Nashville becomes each spring as artists rally for recognition at Gospel Music Week, hoping to keep favor with Christian radio stations and record labels who parade their artists before the promotion gate keepers. It is ironic that a statue of a dove is given out to the winning artist in their respective categories. The dove which symbolizes the unity of the Holy Spirit on one hand, and peace in the world on the other hand, has become a symbol of hierarchy and competition among so many in Christian music.

Even the ranking of songs on Christian radio playlists has become such an obsession that artists and record companies spend thousands of dollars to gain the coveted positions on the top of the charts. (God forgive me for the money I've wasted in this area.)

After years of smuggling Christian music into eastern Europe and the Soviet Union, my heart was broken when the first free Christian radio program told me about their top 20 playlist. Since I had given them the majority of tapes and CDs my song was number one. I was honored and heartbroken at the same time.

Listen carefully! Please hear what I am saying!

There is nothing wrong with promoting our music or artists. There is nothing wrong with wanting to make an honest profit, but this should be in the context of sustaining our business for the cause of ministry, not vice versa.

Our calling should always take precedence over our business. Our calling is to exalt Christ, to magnify Him in a way that people look *beyond* our music and our personalities and see Him alone. This is the challenge of Christian music. It really is the opposite of the world which seeks to exalt itself. Ministry through music across the world is not subject to only what happens in Nashville. God is bigger than that. The CCM industry may not be needed for every music ministry, but for those of us within that industry, we need to discover new ways of promotion with integrity, and recognition without manipulative competition. So much of what the Christian music industry represents is not only antithetical to the Gospel it proclaims, it also cheapens the vessels who proclaim it.

I am not saying that people in the CCM industry do not love Jesus. I have grown up with many people in this industry and hold great respect for their personal devotion to the Lord. I know of a few record labels that have company Bible studies and prayer times led by executives.

Many Christian radio stations begin each day with devotions, and the Gospel Music Association kicks off Gospel Music Week with a worship service. The Gospel Music Association has developed a spiritual input committee to speak into the lives of artists. An 800 prayer hot-line is being developed for artists who desire prayer and counsel, and a prayer chapel is available throughout Gospel Music Week. Great strides are also being made to involve pastors in the lives and ministries of Christian artists as well as in the board rooms of Christian labels.

But even with noble intentions, caught up in the massive machinery of this growing industry, passion for kingdom values can easily be side-lined for the sake of commercial success.

The problem is not that we have Christian record companies, Christian magazines, Christian books, Christian radio or even Christian award shows. ***The problem is when our passion becomes misdirected and how we respond to these commercial channels.*** If these channels *become* the goal, instead of a means towards a greater goal then we are doomed. If they become the criteria for how we define ourselves as Gospel artists then we are only setting ourselves up for failure.

Passion misdirected is when people sell out ministry in order to keep the ministry business going. For example, look at the business of the temple in the Bible (Mark 11:15-17). There was nothing intrinsically wrong with selling doves to pilgrims from North Africa who came to make a sacrifice. This was a ministry service to the believers. The problem was when greed set in among the priests thus allowing business to override ministry.

Now I am a songwriter and recording artist by profession (my occupation). Through album sales, concert income and songwriting royalties I am able to pay my bills. I am also able to sustain my ministry (my vocation or calling) of ministering to the body of Christ through my music which is my "work of service" (Ephesians 4:11).

In a similar way the priest prepared and provided sacrifices for the believers. They made enough profit to sustain their services. Their service was a ministry function and produced even further ministry in the lives of believers. However, it seems greed set in and the focus became their profit rather than their service.

Likewise, as a songwriter and artist, the temptation is to focus on my profit (and recognition) over my ministry service to the body of Christ for the glory of God.

Nehushtan

God instructed Moses to make a bronze serpent and lift it up on a pole before Israel as they journeyed in the wilderness. Everyone who was guilty of sin could look at the bronze serpent and live (Numbers 21:4-8). The serpent itself did not have the power to forgive or give life. It was merely an instrument which pointed to God. It was not an object to be worshiped, but an object to point to the one who was worthy of worship.

Yet by the time of King Hezekiah, the Jews were worshipping the bronze serpent, burning incense to it. Hezekiah wanting to do right in the Lord's eyes, saw the idolatry of Israel, so he took the bronze serpent along with other "religious" articles and smashed them into pieces. The bronze serpent was even called "Nehushtan" which literally means "piece of brass" (2 Kings 18:1-4). Hezekiah is known as the first great reformer of worship at the temple because of his uncompromising devotion to the Lord. He saw that the focus of worship was on the instrument designed to point to God, rather than on God Himself. It was a passion misdirected!

Has this not become an issue in the exaltation of today's Christian artists? Remember that Paul and Barnabas, in Lystra (Acts 14:8-18), tore their clothes and rebuked the people for exalting them as gods after a lame man was healed. They were quick to point to the living God and His power, shouting out, "We too are only men." Paul and Barnabas refused to be worshiped! They knew they were instruments who must point to the only One who is worthy of worship. Could it be that our music and even our ministries have become guilty of being "Nehushtan." Are we competing against God for His own glory? Are we trying to impress people with ourselves or trying to impress them with Jesus?

> "Faith *cannot* co-exist with self exaltation. Faith is inherently humble and God exalting. It always looks from itself to God and delights not in the praises of men, but in the glory of God."[12] - John Piper

> "Every poet and musician and artist, but for grace, is drawn away from love of the thing he tells, to love of the telling, till, down in deep hell, they cannot be interested in God at all, but only in what they say about Him. For it doesn't stop at being interested in paint, you know. They sink lower - become interested in their own personalities and then in nothing but their own reputations."[13] - C.S. Lewis

Consider even the first two commandments where we are explicitly told not to have any other gods before the Lord God, and we must honor and reverence His name. R.C. Sproul states that idolatry is the most fundamental sin of the religious.[14] Anything we trust, exalt or give priority over and above God is idolatry. It is not satisfaction in Christ, but artificial security or satisfaction. It is settling for second rate! Again, Piper says "Sin is what you do when your heart is not satisfied with God."[15]

Do we desire Christ and His kingdom (Rule) over and above talent, ministry, recognition and career? Do we long after God as the deer pants for water? (Psalm 42:1)

How do we respond to God who has called us out of darkness into His wonderful light and separated us into what

He calls a chosen people, a royal priesthood, a holy nation? (1 Peter 2:9)

Can the music industry and the music ministry stand side by side? Should we be career builders or kingdom builders? Can there be integrity in the twentieth century Christian marketplace? Who are the artists God has called and what do they look like? Is there an answer? Is there a hope?

The Kingdom Strikes Back

Ralph Winter, President and founder of the US. Center for World Mission calls Genesis 12 "The Kingdom Strikes Back."[16] Here God called Abram (whom He later called Abraham) and raised him up for a unique purpose in redemptive history:

> "The Lord said to Abram, leave your country, your people and your father's household and go to the land I will show you.
>
> I will make you into a great nation and I will bless you;
>
> I will make your name great, and you will be a blessing.
>
> I will bless those who bless you and whoever curses you I will curse;
>
> And all peoples on earth will be blessed through you" (Genesis 12:1-3).

Theologians call this the Abrahamic Covenant. It was not fake. It was the real thing.

- ⟨ **God** would restore paradise lost - not man.
- ⟨ **God** would make a great nation - not man.
- ⟨ **God** would make their name great and bless them with posterity!

And in the process God's people would be a blessing to all nations. Every tower or pedestal we erect for ourselves to fulfill ourselves falls horribly short of where God desires to take us. Whether it's an album project, a publishing deal, a concert booking, a song on the charts, or our entire career, God has a greater and deeper desire for us that exceeds any temporal satisfaction brought about by our own accomplishments.

God has given us a new name and He rejoices over us! (Isaiah 62:1-5). But with that new name, God has given us a calling to make **His** name great, not ours. He is "jealous for His holy name" (Ezekiel 39:25). Our call is not to the "Hall of Fame" but to the "Hall of Faith!"

The secure rich young ruler was out to make a name for himself. He was probably very well known in his day and knew that he had the world by its tail. But who knows his name today? The writers of the Gospels didn't think it important enough to mention his name even once.

The rich young ruler in his arrogance approached Jesus by saying, "What can I do?" Jesus answered by essentially saying, "You must sell everything you have and give it to the poor where you will never get it back. Only then will you see how bankrupt you are before me and recognize that you cannot do anything of yourself." It is impossible for man to bring anything to the table, even the riches and accomplishments of a rich young ruler. Jesus was saying let God be your wealth and treasure. The rich young ruler had an identity problem. He was focused on his own importance and his own abilities.

Interestingly, just a few verses later in Mark chapter 10, the disciples James and John approached Jesus with a request based on their spiritual accomplishments. They were seeking glorified recognition and position in the kingdom.

It is here that Jesus teaches them the true path to greatness through servanthood and humility "Whoever wants to be great must be the servant of all" (Mark 10:43).

As with the rich young ruler, James and John rooted their identity in their perception of their own importance and what they thought they could bring to the table. Remember, these guys were in the inner circle!

The beauty of this chapter is the concluding story of the blind man of Jericho. As Jesus and His disciples were leaving the city, a blind man named Bartimaeus cried out "Jesus, son of David, have mercy upon me!" (Mark 10:47)

Immediately the blind man received his sight and followed Jesus along the road.

Three requests were made of Jesus: one from a self-reliant rich young ruler, one from spiritually arrogant disciples and one from a broken and humbled blind man who cried out for mercy.

Jesus granted the request of the only one who truly saw his own bankruptcy before God. The rich young ruler and the disciples couldn't see. Their identity was in themselves. Bartimaeus found his identity in Christ and was restored

Restoring Christian Music

God is a God of restoration, and my prayer is that we will see how truly bankrupt we are before God and how much we need his restoration. May we have the courage to cry out for mercy and to look deeply into God's heart for us, our gifts and our calling.

Are we only settling for the low, marshy tarpits of Shinar with a crude tower that reaches to artificial success built on self-determination and self-exaltation? Or are we thirsting for the real thing: the Eden of a rich relationship with the God of Abraham who, as Piper puts it, "is most glorified in us when we are most satisfied in Him."[17]

I am not out to lambaste the Christian Music Industry. For whatever sin I see in this industry, I clearly see in myself as I struggle to be conformed to the image of His son (Romans 8:29) and set my heart on His kingdom and goodness

(Matthew 6:33). Before he preached, the late Jack Miller used to confess to his listeners that he was a recovering Pharisee. Well, I am a recovering "Christian Artist," who has fallen for *all* the lure of fame and fortune. This book first and foremost is for me. It may be for you as well. The good news is that He who has begun a good work in us will complete it until the day of Jesus Christ (Philippians 1:6).

I pray this book will be part of that process.

As the truly classic hymn "Be Thou My Vision" passionately evokes the deepest longing for Christ to be supremely above all things, so may He open our eyes like Bartimaeus and restore our vision.

Be Thou My Vision
>Be Thou my Vision, O Lord of my heart
>Naught be all else to me, save that Thou art
>Thou my best thought, by day or by night
>Waking or sleeping, Thy presence my light.
>
>Be Thou my Wisdom, and Thou my true Word
>I ever with Thee and Thou with me, Lord
>Thou my great Father, I Thy true son
>Thou in me dwelling, and I with Thee one
>
>Riches I heed not, nor man's empty praise
>Thou mine inheritance, now and always
>Thou and Thou only, first in my heart
>High King of heaven, my Treasure Thou art
>
>High King of heaven, my victory won,
>May I reach heaven's joys, O bright heaven's Sun
>Heart of my own heart, whatever befall,
>Still be my Vision, O Ruler of all[19]

This is how we reach the height of heaven's joy and fulfillment. No tower needed!

Chapter Two
Called By Name

Real Christian leaders are people moved at God's pace and in God's time to God's place, not because they fancy themselves there, but because they are drawn.
   - George MacDonald

"Unless the Lord builds the house, it's builders labor in vain" (Psalm 127:1).

Over one thousand years after Babel, another builder stood in the desert before the glory that poured forth from Mount Sinai. Yet what he was about to create was no mere human driven pinnacle of pride. This builder had received a divine commission and a personal calling from the Lord Himself.

"And Moses said to the people of Israel, 'See, the Lord has **called by name Bezalel** the son of Uri, the son of Hur, of the tribe of Judah; **and he has filled him with the spirit of God, with ability, with intelligence, with knowledge, and with all craftsmanship,** to devise artistic designs, to work in gold and silver and bronze, in cutting stone for setting, and in carving wood, for work in every skilled craft. **And he has inspired him to teach**, both him and Oholiab the son of Ahisamach of the tribe of Dan. He has filled them with ability to do every sort of work done by a craftsman or by a designer or by an embroider in blue and purple and scarlet, stuff and fine twined linen, or by a weaver-by any sort of workman or skilled designer. Bezalel and Oholiab and every able man in whom the Lord has put ability and intelligence to know how to do any work in the construction of the sanctuary shall work in accordance with all that the Lord has commanded" (Exodus 35:30-36:1, RSV emphasis added).

In contrast to the Tower of Babel, the tabernacle was designed to bring glory to God alone and to teach His people. It was God inspired, God commissioned and God centered. The tabernacle also served as a glimpse of heavenly things to come (Exodus 25:9-18; Hebrews 8:5). It reflected the dazzling majesty of the creator and infinite God enthroned in beauty and in glory.

Several attributes of Bezalel (the master artist and builder) stand out significantly.

Bezalel was:
1. Called by Name
2. Filled with the Spirit of God,
3. With Ability
4. With Intelligence
5. With Knowledge
6. With all Craftsmanship
7. and inspired to teach

One of the questions I am asked most often by aspiring young musicians and singers is, "How do you make it?" Seminars on Christian music draw thousands of hopefuls each year. Demo tapes and press releases fill an untold number of boxes (not to mention trash cans) of record company offices.

I don't believe I've ever done a concert without someone handing me a cassette of their dreams, urging me to give it a listen or to pass it on to someone in the industry.

And this doesn't only happen in America. The Christian music scene is in full swing all over the world. Christian music seminars are held in South Africa, Europe, Asia, Central America and even more recently in war torn Bosnia. Don't get me wrong. This is not at all bad news. I believe God is raising up an army of faithful artists who will have great impact on the nations. But the question still lingers: Will these artists fall to the Nimrod temptation or aspire to the Bezalel calling? We've talked already about the contemptuousness of Nimrod. Let us look at the attributes of Bezalel and get a closer glimpse of God's heart for the artist.

Called By Name

In the Bible there are three different kinds of calling.

1. A "**general**" call: the general gospel call that goes out to the whole world when the gospel is preached. "Many are called but few are chosen" (Matthew 22:14, NASB).

2. An "**effectual**" call: the effective inner call whereby God quickens our heart (Ephesians 2:5) and by His gift of faith we are justified (Romans 5:1).

3. A "**specific**" call: To serve as Apostles, prophets, evangelists, pastors, teachers (Ephesians 4:11-12) with specific gifts (Romans 12:4-8; 1 Corinthians 12:4-11) or with "common gifts and talents" - the natural ability to do something. (John Calvin called these "gifts of common grace.") These "common gifts" are not limited to God's people only but are vocational callings.

Bezalel was called specifically by name for a specific task. It was not a general calling but a personal, special calling by God Himself.

The prophet Jeremiah received a specific call before he was even born! "Before I formed you in the womb I knew you, before you were born I *set you apart*; I *appointed you* as a prophet to the nations" (Jeremiah 1:5 emphasis added).

In Acts 9:15 God told Ananias that Paul "is my *chosen instrument* to carry my name before the Gentiles and their kings and before the people of Israel." This was a specific call on Paul's life, and he defended it with a passion.

Look how Paul opens his letters:

Romans: "Paul, a servant of Christ Jesus, called to be an apostle, and set apart for the Gospel of God."

1 Corinthians: "Paul, called to be an apostle of Christ Jesus."

2 Corinthians: "Paul, an apostle of Christ Jesus by the will of God."

Galatians: "Paul, an apostle - sent not from men nor by man but by Jesus Christ." (first two chapters defend this)

Ephesians: "Paul, an apostle of Christ Jesus by the will of God."

Philippians: "Servants of Christ Jesus." (with Timothy)

Colossians: "by the will of God."

1 Timothy: "by the command of God."

2 Timothy: "by the will of God."

Titus: "entrusted to me by the command of God."

Philemon: "Paul, a prisoner of Christ Jesus."

Jeremiah was called before he was born. Paul was called by the command of God. Bezalel was called by name. It doesn't get anymore personal than that.

But what about you and me? Should we wait for a blinding light or a proclamation from on high? Is God limited to these dramatic ways of calling.

Let me suggest four gauges by which we can better understand and affirm our own calling:

1. **Our hearts are stirred:**

It is not unusual for us to sense a stirring in our hearts to serve the Lord in a way that is pleasing to us. If we enjoy singing or playing an instrument then it is only natural that we would lean towards involvement in a musical expression of our faith in service to God. The Apostle Paul urges us to fulfill our giftings with joy and enthusiasm (Romans 12). Whether this is on a professional level or not, we are meant to enjoy our talents and giftings in our service to God. We are actually fulfilled in doing so.

Exodus 36:2 (NASB) speaks of all those whose "hearts were stirred" to come and do the work. It did qualify the invitation by calling upon skilled men, but the implication revealed that there was an excitement that stirred their hearts to be a part of what God was doing!

2. **Sober estimate of ourselves:**

Romans 12:3 states: "Do not think of yourselves more highly than you ought, but rather think of yourself with sober judgment, in accordance with the measure of faith God has given you." The Jewish New Testament renders this same verse "not to have exaggerated ideas about your own importance. Instead, develop a sober estimate of yourself."

All Christians are called to worship, but having sober estimates of themselves, many Christians realize they are not called to be worship leaders. All Christians are called to evangelize but not all Christians are called to be evangelists. The logic is simple.

Over-exaggerated ideas about our abilities can bring tremendous frustration and disillusionment into our ministries.

I am only 5 feet 6 inches tall. It is obvious to me that no matter how much I love basketball, I am not physically equipped to head out for the NBA. God equips us when He calls us. "For we are God's workmanship, created in Christ Jesus to do good works, which God prepared in advance for us to do." (Ephesians 2:10) We have been prepared by God through His people for works of service (Ephesians 4:12) and equipped by Christ with every good thing for doing his will (Hebrews 13:21).

3. Confirmation of others:

King David's skill, gifting and anointing was recognized by Saul's servant in his impressive recommendation of the harp player to the King (1 Samuel 16:18). Paul's calling to be an ambassador to the Gentiles was confirmed by the Apostles and elders in Acts 15. Timothy's gift was affirmed by the elders as Paul reminded him in I Timothy 4:14. It has been said that "Your gift will make room for you". In other words your gift will open doors of opportunity for you to minister as others (especially church leadership) recognize and affirm them in you.

4. Lasting fruit:

In John 15:16 Jesus says "You did not choose me, but I choose you to go and bear fruit - fruit that will last." This "lasting fruit" is consistent with our "good works" (Ephesians 2:10) and our specific giftings (Romans 12:6-8; I Corinthians 12:7-11) in accordance to our office or calling in the church (Ephesians 4:11-12). Our "talents" work in harmony with our giftings and calling to produce lasting results for the Kingdom. We must be careful to never confuse commercial success with Kingdom success, although both may be evident at the same time.

These four gauges are not intended to put God in a box. Obviously, He can use anyone at anytime for any purpose He desires. He can raise up a person "for such a time as this" to accomplish His will.

He can even speak through a donkey for that matter! But for us to consider a "life calling" we must be willing to examine ourselves with scrutiny.

There is a saying "God doesn't call those who are qualified, He qualifies those He calls". This may be true but it in no way negates our commitment to preparation.

If anything is detrimental to the Christian music ministry, it is an attitude of bypassing the process to get to the product. But God is as interested in the process as He is the product. He is more concerned with our character than our career! Remember, God told Noah to build an ark and then waited over a hundred years to send the flood!

When George Muller was a young man starting out in ministry, he sensed a deep call to be an evangelist. But after many unsuccessful services in his twenties, he decided that God had other plans for him. It was heart breaking, but being a man devoted to the Lord, Muller continued to serve God by helping orphans. For decades he selflessly gave his life to building orphanages throughout England.

By the time Muller was 67 he had earned such a platform of respect and honor that his preaching was in high demand and sent him thousands of miles proclaiming the Gospel. He is known as one of the nineteenth century's foremost Christian statesmen. George Muller was a man who operated not out of a sense of drivenness, but out of a sense of calling. He trusted God enough to lay down his dream and go through the process, where ever God should lead.

The writer George MacDonald has said that "real Christian leaders are people who are moved at God's pace and in God's time to God's place, not because they fancy themselves there, but because they are drawn."[1]

Genuine leaders operate out of a sense of calling, not a sense of drivenness. So many aspiring artists just can't wait to get their album out. Even some Christian companies have formed groups to capitalize on a certain sound or style and released records on unseasoned musicians let alone unseasoned ministries. They have metaphorically "laid hands" on these artists and given them a platform for which they may not be ready says Darrell Harris, founder of STAR SONG Records, chaplain of the Gospel Music Association.

Consider the disasters of several secular pop artists whom the Christian music industry thrust out there when they could barely walk in the spiritual sense. They sold a lot of records but their immaturity as babes in Christ gave way to the squeeze of the world.

"He must not be a recent convert, or he may become conceited and fall under the same judgement as the devil" (1 Timothy 3:6). Although this is in reference to the office of Deacons and Overseers in the church, it would be prudent advice for anyone desiring a platform in Christian music.

Worship leader and music missionary Karen Lafferty points out, "An album should be the fruit of a ministry, not the seed of it".

Consider the Hebrew words that were used for the word *"appointment"* as the singers were appointed to musical guilds under King David.

1. *Hibediyl* (1 Chronicles 25:1) means separated as if by a fence. The musicians were appointed (along with the commanders of the army) into the Abodah (service) which refers to serving in the sense of a slave or trusted steward. These musicians would be engaged in warfare, so David conferred with the commanders of the army. In Psalm 144 David sings "Praise be to the Lord my rock who trains my hands for war, my fingers for battle."

2. *He emythal* (1 Chronicles 15 and 16) means a legal agreement, to impose a law on someone with grave penalties for breaking what they considered a contract with God.

3. *Natan* (1 Chronicles 16:4,7) means given over into the custody and empowering of God.

The call to ministry must be a higher, more scrutinized call than a common call to pure entertainment in music. Character (and skill, which we will look at later) is of utmost importance. The process of God's preparation will produce the kind of Godly character needed for effective, impacting ministry. Don't begrudge the process. It has been said that God took Moses through the palace in order to use him in the desert, and God took Joseph through the desert in order to use him in the palace.

You may be in the desert process or the palace process. God may keep you in the desert because this is where you will bring Him the greatest glory. The palace may not be where you would be most effective. Don't despise those who are in the palace. They are there for God's purposes. They may or may not stay there. But this is not your business, it is God's. Oh how I have struggled on this one. "It is harder to deal with other's successes than it is their failures," says Pastor Jim Cymbala of The Brooklyn Tabernacle Choir.

> *God took Moses through the palace in order to use him in the desert, and God took Joseph through the desert in order to use him in the palace.*

We need to keep our eyes on ourselves and put our full trust and confidence in "Him who is able to do immeasurably more than all we ask or imagine, according to his power that is at work within us" (Ephesians 3:20).

Are you in the wilderness now? Listen:

"The desert and the parched land will be glad; the wilderness will rejoice and blossom. Like the crocus, it will burst into bloom; it will rejoice greatly and shout for joy. The glory of Lebanon will be given to it, the splendor of Carmel and Sharon; they will see the glory of the LORD, the splendor of our God." (Isaiah 35:1-2).

God will do immeasurably more in our lives because it will bring Him greater glory!

God has called all of us for the praise of His glorious grace. (Ephesians 1:6) This is our destiny as His adopted sons.

He will conform us to the image of His son. (Romans 8:29) The desert shall bloom!

As we look more closely at Bezalel's attributes we will see what much of that conforming grace is all about.

G.D. Watson a Wesleyan Methodist minister, evangelist and missionary (1845-1924) wrote these rich words that speak to me so often when I loose sight of God's jealous love for me:

Others May, You Cannot

"If God has called you to be really like Jesus, He will draw you to a life of crucifixion and humility, and put upon you such demands of obedience, that you will not be able to follow other people, or measure yourself by other Christians, and in many ways He will seem to let other good people do things which He will not let you do.

"Other Christians and ministers who seem very religious and useful may push themselves, pull wires, and work schemes to carry out their plans, but you cannot do it; and if you attempt it, you will meet with such failure and rebuke from the Lord as to make you sorely penitent.

"Others may boast of themselves, of their work, of their success, of their writings, but the Holy Spirit will not allow you to do any such thing, and if you begin it, He will lead you into some deep mortification that will make you despise yourself and all your good works.

"Others may be allowed to succeed in making money, or may have a legacy left to them, but is likely God will keep you poor, because He wants you to have something far better than gold, namely, a helpless dependence on Him, that He may have the privilege of supplying your needs day by day out of an unseen treasury.

"The Lord may let others be honored and put forward, and keep you hidden in obscurity, because He wants you to produce some choice, fragrant fruit for His coming glory, which can only be produced in the shade. He may let others be great, but keep you small. He may let others do a work for Him and get the credit for it, but He will make you work and toil on without knowing how much you are doing; and then to make your work still more precious, He may let others get the credit for the work which you have done, and thus make your reward ten times greater when Jesus comes.

"The Holy Spirit will put a strict watch over you, with a jealous love, and will rebuke you for little words and feelings, or for wasting your time, which other Christians never seem distressed over. So make up your mind that God is an infinite Sovereign, and has a right to do as He pleases with His own.

"He may not explain to you a thousand things which puzzle your reason in His dealings with you. But if you absolutely sell yourself to be His...slave, he will wrap you up in a jealous love, and bestow upon you many blessings which come only to those who are in the inner circle.

"Settle it forever, then, that you are to deal directly with the Holy Spirit, and that He is to have the privilege of tying your tongue, or chaining your hand, or closing your eyes, in ways that He does not seem to use with others. Now when you are so possessed with the living God that you are, in your secret heart, pleased and delighted over this peculiar, personal, private, jealous guardianship and management of the Holy Spirit over your life, you will have found the vestibule of Heaven."[2]

Listening

Finally, we must master the art of listening to God. Have you listened to God, to hear His heart regarding the specific call upon your life? Sometimes we are so busy making our own plans, God can hardly get a word in edgewise.

After Paul's dramatic encounter with the Lord on the road to Damascus, he spent 3 days in blind stillness waiting on the Lord. I am certain he was listening keenly for God to speak which eventually happened through the Lord's servant Ananias.

It is a safe bet that in the midst of heaven's throne and a temple filled with holy smoke the ears of Isaiah's heart were finely tuned to God's commission (Isaiah 6).

"Guard your steps when you go to the house of God. Go near to listen." (Ecclesiastes 5:1). It may sound too simple, but we need to listen.

Assignment and Alignment

Pastor Dale Evrist of New Song Christian Fellowship in Nashville has said that in order to be successful in our calling we must discover "our proper assignment and our proper alignment."

In other words, we must know what specific focus the Lord has for us and what specific people we are to link up with who will validate, support, and facilitate us because they share the same focus.

In the world today, people are looking for "specialists," not "generalists." Likewise the church needs "specialists." That is why some are called as apostles, prophets, evangelists, pastors and teachers. (Ephesians 4:11) or have ministries of mercy (Romans 12:8).

You may sense the Lord calling you to be in music ministry. But what is your specialty? Unfortunately many Christian artists struggle in defining the specific nature of their calling. Many artists end up wandering from one cause to another, one look to another, even one sound to another.

I've heard many artists say the record company is going to model them after so and so in the secular music scene. Other artists tell me they've been bounced around from one trend to the next by agents, managers, and producers.

All of this is called "positioning." It is how your audience will perceive you. It is your image. You better understand this, especially if you are pursuing a market place/ministry career. If you don't know your identity coming in, you may never know it coming out. I know of several artists who struggle with confusion over their identity and image now that the contract is over. If you don't "position yourself," others will do it for you. It may not be consistent with the calling God has given to you.

Positioning ourselves properly comes out of a solid understanding of what the Lord's assignment is for us. Are we teachers or evangelists? Are we gearing to teenagers or to adults? Is our appearance slick and flashy or homespun? What is the theme of our presentation or the focus of our songs? Are we to minister in our local church or are we to minister nationally or even internationally?

We need to evaluate and pray over these questions. Obviously having a "sane estimate of our capabilities" (Romans 12:3) and the confirmation of others helps us realize our assignment (1 Timothy 4:14).

Often times, once we establish our position it sticks forever. Madonna will always be looked at as rebellious, extravagant, and immoral no matter what she does! Even her convincing role in the movie *Evita* could not wash away peoples' perception of her.

Politicians spend millions to position themselves. What President doesn't have a picture of himself kissing a baby?

For the Christian artist this goes much deeper than the slick rhetoric of press releases and glossy photos. Good "positioning" is being in the right place before the Lord, even if it cuts across the grain of your career.

My specific call is teaching, missions mobilization, and worship. This is the grid by which I make all decisions concerning my ministry. Unless the Lord were to lead me otherwise, the only ministry opportunities I accept must fall within these parameters. This keeps me in focus and on track with my assignment.

The Apostle Paul knew his specific call. He even defended that call before the elders in Acts 15. Paul had a vision and assignment from the Lord and was faithful to keep that focus to the end.

It is true that without a vision the people perish. (Proverbs 29:18 KJV) Another translation states that "the people are unrestrained" (NASB). The Hebrew picture is one of running aimlessly while letting an opportunity slip through the fingers. Knowing our assignment and being in the right position helps us avoid running aimlessly and missing the real opportunity to accomplish what God has called us to do no matter where we are in our careers.

The specific assignment God gives to us is never to be contingent upon the gift He gives to us. If my fingers get cut off and I can never play the guitar again, that doesn't mean that I will no longer write or lead worship or mobilize for missions. My passion will not change.

> *Our calling is higher than our gift.*
> *Our gifts are not an end unto themselves,*
> *but a means to a greater end.*

Research has shown that most popular artists have about a six year window of high profile in the marketplace. A ministry assignment does not end with the termination of the contract. If anything, it should release the artist into new dimensions of that assignment.

Eventually the marketplace passes everyone by. If the Christian artist's vision and goals rest solely on marketplace success, then he will face ultimate failure. If his vision and goals rest in the context of his assignment then he will continue on with a new set of dynamics.

Actually, many artists who never enter into the marketplace of the Christian music industry enjoy long, successful, and satisfying careers because their focus is not based on the whims and trends of the buying public but on an entirely different paradigm of ministry.

In the marketplace the criteria for affirmation and success is based on commercial viability. The danger is that *most artists* are only "momentarily marketable." It's a shaky foundation for a career and has very little to do with Kingdom purposes because the focus is *"You"*. When *"You"* are no longer marketable, you will see your career as being over.

The ministry paradigm means focusing on the Kingdom and not *our* careers. *Our* careers no matter what stage they are in, are always focused on the larger issue of the Kingdom.

Therefore the aspiration is to become a full time servant who is willing to serve in any way to get the job done. If notoriety comes, it is the servant of the master plan. If there is no recognition, the master plan remains intact. This goes along with Paul's words to Timothy "Preach the Word; be prepared in season and out of season" (2 Timothy 4:2). The focus is the Kingdom, not the circumstances of the preacher. I love the saying "The main thing is keeping the main thing the main thing!"

For *us* the **main thing** is God's glory and kingdom rule. *Our* gifts are not the main thing.

Back when the airlines were a fledgling little industry, the train companies laughed because they knew, at the time, that trains were the main thing. They did not see "transportation of people and products" as the main thing. They focused on the tool and not the purpose. In the end they lost most of the market because people were not interested in trains. They were interested in transportation. The airline industry has proven that.

If our vision as Christian artists is focused on ourselves, our careers or our gifts, then we are headed down tracks that wander aimlessly to no where. If there is no understanding of our proper assignment, then all that we attempt to do won't make any sense. There's an old saying *"if you aim at nothing, you'll hit it every time."*

What are you aiming at? What is your assignment?

Is it bigger than you? Or is your career overshadowing it?

Byron Spradlin of ACT (Artists In Christian Testimony) states that the market-based paradigm is not adequate enough to sustain a ministry. A ministry based paradigm however is adequate enough to sustain itself "in and out of season." Byron has offered us what the ministry based paradigm looks like as compared to the marketplace paradigm.

MINISTRY	MARKETPLACE
˘ Aspire to be a servant	˘ Aspire to be successful
˘ Success based on God's promise	˘ Success based on commercial viability
˘ Affirmation based out of a call from God and confirmed by service development and ministry	˘ Affirmation based on product
˘ All Christian artists including volunteer artists or bi-vocational can have validity	˘ Only commercially successful have validity

This is not to say there is not some cross-over between these two paradigms. Understanding our proper assignment can help us put marketplace values in a Kingdom context and strengthen commitment to core ministry values. The ministry paradigm can then be supplemented by a healthier marketplace if needed.

In the next chapter I will discuss the need for proper alignment with those who will validate, support, and facilitate the artist in his calling.

In Review: 10 Steps

1. Know that you have been prepared by God for works of service (Ephesians 4:12) and equipped to do His will (Hebrews 13:21).
2. Seek to understand your divine appointment and proper assignment (Ephesians 2:10; see Jeremiah's calling, Jeremiah 1:5).
3. Have a sane estimate of your capabilities (Romans 12:3). (They should line up with your assignment.)
4. Seek the affirmation of others in leadership that this is your gift (1 Timothy 4:14).
5. Ask the Lord to help you develop a missions statement (Habakkuk 2:2-3 - write down the vision).
6. Develop a ministry support team (discussed in chapter three).
7. Don't despise the process (Philippians 1:6).
8. Don't be anxious for the product (James 5:7-11).
9. Listen (Ecclesiastes 5:1).
10. Look for the fruit (John 15:16; Ephesains 2:10; Romans 12:6-8).

Chapter Three

Filled With the Spirit of God

They will be called oaks of righteousness, a planting of the Lord for the display of His splendor.
　- Isaiah 61:3

When I was in college I served as a volunteer leader for a high school ministry called Young Life. Once a week we held a "club" meeting in the home of one of the high school kids who was involved with the program. The three of us who led the club were Skip, John, and myself. Skip was the Area Director for Young Life and had started the ministry in this particular high school. He was a brilliant theologian and speaker with a seminary education. His stirring Gospel messages at the end of each club meeting made me want to accept Christ all over again.

John was a local college student who was quiet, yet friendly. He didn't have much talent in the speaking or singing department. He basically just hung around with the kids. On the other hand, I was given charge over the song leading and cherished every moment I could razzle and dazzle the kids with my newest guitar riffs. I felt confident whenever I spoke in front of the club and could be real funny in the crazy skits we performed each night.

John seemed to stumble through his words, and he wasn't very funny in the skits.

Young Life was the ultimate for me, and I was convinced when our leader Skip left to start a new club in another high school, he would leave me in charge of the existing club.

The reasons were all obvious. I could lead singing. I could be funny in the skits. I could give a good Gospel message and invitation. But when Skip made his final decision he chose John. I had to gasp for air. I couldn't believe it. And when I asked Skip for a reason, what he told me has echoed in my heart time and time again.

"John wants to want to love Jesus" was Skip's answer. I looked stunned.

He repeated it again "John wants to want to love Jesus." And then he said, "Chew on it, Scott." I've been chewing on it ever since!

What does it mean to want to want to love Jesus? What was it in my friend John that Skip chose over my ability and talent? Perhaps this is why, after God called Bezalel by name, the first attribute given is that **he was filled with the Spirit of God**. I believe this is foundational to all else. It comes before talent and ability. It doesn't negate talent and ability, but prioritizes the "effectual calling" where there is relationship *with* God over the "vocational calling" where there is service *to* God.

The Bible describes Bezalel, an artist, as the first person being filled with God's Spirit. This is what distinguished him from other talented artists and craftsmen of his day: "God's presence!" In Exodus 33, Moses didn't want to proceed into the Promised Land unless God's presence went with Israel.

> "Then Moses said to Him (God); If your presence does not go with us, do not send us up from here. How will anyone know that you are pleased with me and with Your people unless You go with us. WHAT WILL DISTINGUISH ME AND YOUR PEOPLE from all the other people on the face of this earth?" (Exodus 33:15-16, emphasis added, NIV)

The Power of God's Presence

God's presence distinguishes Christian artists from all the other artists on the face of this earth. No amount of strength, talent, or human charisma can replace the impact of God's presence. If we are not in God's presence, we will never be able to operate in the full capacity of God's power.

Remember what happened to Samson when he went out not knowing the Lord had departed from him? (Judges 16:20) The Philistines seized him, gouged out his eyes and bound him up in shackles in prison. Samson was operating against the enemy in his own strength, not the Lord's. What happens if we go out on our stage of ministry in our own strength? Perhaps that is much of the problem for some Christian artists today. Often the enemy blinds our eyes and binds us in the shackles of commercialism, materialism, unhealthy competition and comparison, and undisciplined lives.

We have lusted after the attractiveness of worldly success, and in the process we have forgotten our mission.

Samson forgot his mission because he was blinded by his lust for the attractiveness of Delilah. Ultimately, blinded by God, Samson could see nothing else but God's plan. He realized his true strength was in the power of God's presence. It was a painful lesson to learn. I pray it will not be as painful for those of us in Christian music.

The **Relationships** of God's Presence

Howard Hendricks says "Our lives and our ministries are inseparably related so the closeness of our walk with Christ will determine how effectively we communicate His message."[1] On a recent TV movie on the life of Frank Sinatra I noticed how the insensitivity of the press pushed Mr. Sinatra to violent acts of retribution. After punching out one reporter for questioning him on a recent divorce, Frank Sinatra said "All I owe you is a good show!"

But is that all we owe people? A good show?

I think it's much more! What people see on stage is just the surface, the public personae. Ninety-five percent of who we truly are is underneath. It is that off-stage character and our willingness to be accountable that matters most. Bill Hybels captures the essence of my point in the title of his book, *Who Are You When Nobody is Looking?*

Os Guinness says "A man should walk before God, before he walks before men."[2]

King David was a man after God's own heart. He was strong, he was talented, but his hearts desire was to know God. When Samuel anointed David (1 Samuel 16:12-13) the Bible says the Spirit of the Lord came mightily upon him, FROM THAT DAY FORWARD. All of the musicians and singers that David appointed for the ministry at the house of God were under the supervision of their fathers Asaph, Jeduthum and Heman who in turn were under the supervision of the King (1 Chronicles 25:1-6). King David himself was accountable to Samuel, Nathan, and Gad as representatives of the Lord. This brings into sharp focus the need for Christian artists to be accountable to their elders. It doesn't mean that you are told what to sing and what to wear in concert (although that might be a good idea for some artists).

Rather, it is a biblical model for ministry. I have always been accountable to a church, pastor, and elders or mission board since I began my ministry in 1973. Every struggle I have faced, and practically every decision I have made, has been submitted for prayer and consultation. I cannot imagine facing all that alone.

> "Without consultation plans are frustrated. But with many counselors they succeed" (Prov 15:22).

Are you frustrated? Are you grounded in solid fellowship which is *concerned more for your heart than your art?* Are you blessed?

> "Blessed is the man who does not walk in the counsel of the wicked or stand in the way of sinners or sit

in the seat of mockers. [A place or position of influence] But his delight is in the law of the Lord, and on His law he meditates day and night. He is like a tree planted by streams of water, which yields its fruit in season and whose leaf does not wither. Whatever he does prospers." (Psalm 1:1-3, clarification added, NIV)

We are called to walk in the counsel of the wise and godly men and women in our lives, and to meditate (dwell) upon God's word day and night.

Once again, Pastor Dale Evrist states in order to be truly successful in our ministries we must understand *the proper assignment and proper alignment* of our calling. We have already discussed understanding our specific assignment in chapter two. Now we need to ask who has God called to stand with us as Godly counsel? Are we operating in the context of a proper alignment with our pastors, elders or ministry board?

Several artists in Nashville (including myself) have a board of directors over their ministry.

Again these boards are not set up to smother or control an artist, but to stand with him in encouragement, challenge and prayer. They are both ministry partners and business advisors.

In developing a ministry board or support team, ask the Lord to knit you together with mature Christians who:

T. You can *Trust* with with your hopes and dreams, frustrations and failures.

E. Will *Encourage* you and affirm your gifts and calling.

A. Will hold you *Accountable* to your ministry standards *and* personal walk with Christ.

M. Will help you keep your *Mission* and vision in focus.

I am also a part of a small men's accountability group from my church that meets every Thursday morning. These dear brothers are such a great source of encouragement and challenge to me in my walk with the Lord and my public ministry. They are my prayer partners and my personal system of checks and balances.

Having a system of checks and balances for our lives and ministries is so critical to developing a deep, long lasting impact. Somewhere Shakespeare has said, "all that glitters is not gold."[3] What can distinguish Christian artists from other artists, is that behind that glitter there is true gold!

Accountability is part of the gold-refining process. If you are a Lone Ranger Christian artist, you may be headed for serious trouble. Most of the recent "Television evangelist" disasters were a result of the "no accountability factor." Some of that has crept into Christian music and taken it's toll on several well known artists!

The June 1996 issue of *Christianity Today* magazine quoted Stan Moser former CEO of Star Song Records saying, "There is a growing chasm between CCM and the church–between what's actually happening in the real world of ministry, or even in the music ministry of the church, and what we're doing in CCM." Just two pages earlier, Michael Card stated "There's a big accountability gap in the (CCM) industry as a result of a lack of connectedness to the church."[4]

At the foundation of this gap between the industry and the church, there is a gap between the artist and the church. Until artists are willing to submit to the wisdom, counsel and discipline of the church we can expect no accountability on the part of the industry at large.

The **Character** of God's Presence

"Who may ascend the hill of the Lord?
Who may stand in his holy place?

He who has **clean hands** and **a pure heart,** who
does not lift up his soul to an idol or **swear by
what is false.**
He will receive blessing from the Lord
and vindication from God his Savior.
Such is the generation of those who seek Him,
who seek your face, O God of Jacob"
(Psalm 24:3-6, emphasis added, NIV)

This beautiful psalm of David was sung by the Temple
singers at the beginning of each week. It exemplifies the kind
of character that is required for the Lord's servants as His
musicians. It is the gold behind the glitter of our performance.
So let's ask some tough, "gold-refining" questions about the
way we conduct our ministries.

Clean Hands

Paul exhorts us to lift up holy hands (1 Timothy 2:8).
How do we deal with our hands in the business of Christian
music?

Are we honest with our handshake or the drafting of our
contracts?

Do we take advantage of others in unethical ways? Do
we pursue righteous dealings?

Moses and Aaron were commanded by the Lord to wash
their hands and feet before they could even approach the
altar in the Tent of Meeting (Exodus 40:30-32).

Do we approach the altar with a clear conscience before God and men? (Acts 24:16).

What kind of lives do we live off the stage of our ministry? Do we show up at an engagement with dirty hands from
a dirty lifestyle and ask God to bless the concert just before
we go on? Do we travel the Path of Righteousness?" (Psalm
23:3).

Recently a church mistakenly overpaid me for a concert I had given. A deposit was originally sent to me, but apparently was never recorded on their books. When I questioned them about the additional money they were certain that they owed me the full amount of the honorarium. As much as I needed that extra money I knew that it would be wrong to take advantage of their bookkeeping error. The temptation was there. I needed to ask God for a "clean-hands" attitude because in my flesh I was trying to justify keeping the money. No one would ever know – except God and me.

In financially stressful times the core issue is not so much an issue of honesty, but rather an issue of trust. Did I trust God enough to meet all of my needs or was I going to dishonestly help Him out a little? John Piper says "the failure to believe God is the root cause of rebelling against His command."[5]

"You shall not steal" is His command. (Exodus 20:15)

"Trust in the Lord and do good." (Psalm 37:3)

Doing good or doing the right thing is because there is trust in the Lord.

I knew God saw my financial situation and that the extra money would have helped so much. But it wasn't mine. It belonged to the church. Certainly God would meet all my needs according to His riches in glory in Christ Jesus! (Philippians 4:14)

Piper again says that "all my needs" means "all that I need for God-glorifying contentment"[6] Our hands are clean when we content ourselves with all God is for us. Our trust in Him leads us to obedience and doing good, even when things appear to be bleak. The week I mailed that check back to the church for the overage was the week I received a higher than usual royalty check! Much higher than the money I could have dishonestly kept. But even if I hadn't received any royalties the reward of having clean hands and honoring the Lord would have been enough!

"Incline my heart to thy testimonies and not to dishonest gain," (Psalm 119:36) **because,** "There is great gain in godliness combined with contentment" (1 Timothy 6:6 NRSV).

"And God is able to make all grace abound to you, that always having all sufficiency in everything, you may have an abundance for every good deed" (2 Corinthians 9:8, NASB).

Pure Heart

Jesus said "Blessed are the pure in heart, for they will see God" (Matthew 5:8) Can we see God in our lives and ministries? Can we see His Kingdom and righteousness more than our own determination for fame and fortune? Do we desire his desires and surrender our motives to His motives?

This is what I believe it means to let our lights shine, IN SUCH A WAY, that others see our good works, yet glorify our Father in heaven (Matthew 5:16). A pure heart is a heart that is satisfied in seeing God receive all the glory whether we are remembered or not.

In his letter to the Ephesians, the Apostle Paul paints a sharp contrast between walking in darkness and walking in the light. He exhorts us not to be partakers with those who walk in darkness but "instead, be filled with the Spirit." (Ephesians 5:18, NIV)

It is interesting that most of us musicians will go on to quote the following verses "Speak to one another with psalms, hymns and spiritual songs. Sing and make music in your heart to the Lord (most of us drop out here) always giving thanks to God the father for everything (a little tougher to do) in the name of our Lord Jesus Christ" (verses 19, 20; comments added, NIV).

But it gets much more involved as we go onto the more weightier verses that deal with submission to one another, loving each other as Christ (sacrificially) loved the Church, honoring those in authority over us and not lording it over those in positions below us. (Ephesians 5:21-6:9) Being filled with the Spirit in Paul's mind goes far beyond the physical expression of music. Rather it reflects an entire life-style.

Does Not Lift Up His Soul to an Idol

Webster's New World Dictionary defines "idol" as an image of a god or any object of ardent or excessive devotion or admiration.[7] *The Chambers Twentieth Century Dictionary* renders "an object of love, admiration, or honor in an extreme degree" and also implies that an idol is a FALSE object, not worthy of such admiration.[8] The footnotes of the *New American Standard Bible* indicate the meaning of "idol," which is translated "falsehood" as lifting up our souls in vain.[9]

Is it possible that we could be our own idols? I shudder when I hear the words "Christian stars." But that is exactly where so much of the focus is in Christian music today. Career issues become more important than Kingdom issues. Are we guilty of making career moves over Kingdom moves? Do we lift up our soul to the idol of our own image and career with excessive devotion or admiration. As Bob Dylan sang "You gotta serve somebody." Who do we serve?

Remember, the Temple singers who sang this Psalm had signed a contract with God in the Hebrew legal sense. (We will look later at what happened when this system collapsed).

Do we lift up our soul to the success syndrome of today's humanistic world? Do we allow others to exalt us and put us on a pedestal where instead of serving them we ourselves are served. Do we demand to be treated as special, or as stars? Maybe you're not there yet, but is that a part of your goal, hidden deep inside your soul? Are the bright lights and all the newest, hippest equipment, big concert halls, huge product sales, charting songs and public recognition the things which define your idea of success in Christian music?

Does Not Swear by What is False

Maybe this is where our "Press Release" comes in. Are we "bigger than life" in what is printed about us? What about exaggerated reports of record sales or concert attendance? Do we speak "evang-elastic-ally?"

"He who speaks truth declares righteousness, but a false witness, deceit. There is one who speaks like the piercings of a sword, but the tongue of the wise **promotes** health. The truthful lip shall be **established forever.** But a lying tongue is but for the moment...Lying lips are an abomination to the Lord, But those who deal truth-fully are His delight." (Proverbs 12:17-22)

Do we put other artists down to elevate ourselves? Remember it is easier to deal with other people's failures than their success. Do we try to belittle the accomplishments of others to make ourselves feel and look better? "It ruined King Saul's day to see David succeed," says Pastor Jim Cymbala. Saul went as far as trying to kill David. Do we try to kill others with our discrediting words, while promoting ourselves with exaggeration? "Therefore, laying aside falsehood, speak truth, each one of you, with his neighbor." (Ephesians 4:25 NASB)

He Will Receive Blessings From the Lord

Jerry White in his book *Honesty, Morality and Conscience* says, "Ethics to the government is Law. Ethics to the philosopher is concept. Ethics to religion is morality. But ethics to God is obedience."[10]

The psalmist was calling the Temple singers into accountability. Psalm 24 was a code of honor. It was also a promise of blessing for the obedience of those who not just sang it, but lived it. The Bible promises reward for obedience (Leviticus 26, Proverbs 11:18; 13:21; Jeremiah 17:10; Matthew 6:4; 10:41; Ephesians 6:8; Hebrews 11; Revelation 22:12).

> "Finally, brothers, whatever is true, whatever is noble, whatever is right, whatever is pure, whatever is lovely, whatever is admirable - if anything is excellent or praiseworthy - think about such things. Whatever you have learned or received or heard from me, or seen in me - **put it into practice.** And the God of peace will be with you."
> (Philippians.4:8-9, emphasis added, NIV)

Such is the generation of artists who seek Him. The fruit of honesty, integrity and righteousness are supported by the deep roots of "being filled with the Spirit of God."

Like the foundation of a tall building goes several stories deep, so must the foundation of our lives and ministries. (Luke 6:46-49) When the flood of the world's temptations come against us, we will not be shaken. Our blessing will be our delight in Christ.

> "The Law of the Lord is perfect, reviving the soul.
> The statutes of the Lord are trustworthy, making wise the simple.
> The precepts of the Lord are right, giving joy to the heart.
> The fear of the Lord is pure, enduring forever.
> The ordinances of the Lord are sure and altogether righteous.
> They are more precious than gold...sweeter than honey."
> (Psalm 19:7-10 NIV)

Here's a simple chart which illustrates the rewards we receive when we desire the things of God "more than gold":

God's law	Perfect	Revives our soul
God's statutes	Trustworthy	Makes us wise
God's precepts	Right	Gives joy to our hearts
God's commands	Radiant	Gives light to our eyes
Godly fear	Pure	Helps us endure
God's ordinances	Sure	We grow in righteousness

King David wrote Psalm 19 to the Chief Musician. See it as a reminder of God's heart to revive Christian music, and raise up wise, joyful servants who see what God is doing, who resist the world which tries to squeeze us into its own mold, and who demonstrate God's righteousness in our music and our lives.

None of this is legalism. It is liberating grace. It is truth. It is the discipline of grace that will distinguish Christian artists from all the other artists on the face of this earth. But we are not alone in this pursuit. As Jerry Bridges analogizes "Think of the two wings of the airplane: discipline and dependence. This airplane illustrates one of the most important principles in the Christian life. Just as the airplane must have both wings to fly, so we must exercise both discipline and dependence in the pursuit of holiness."[11]

Although Paul exhorts us to "train ourselves" (I Tim. 4:7), we cannot do it in our own strength and determination. We must depend on the Holy Spirit, and He is more than willing!

A Priestly Calling

The ultimate goal of all ministry is God's glory. This is why he leads us in paths of righteousness. It is for His name's sake! (Psalm 23:3) He has chosen us and called us a royal priesthood, a holy nation and a people belonging to God that *we might declare His praises!* (1 Peter 2:9; Exodus 19:6)

The Hebrew word for priest, *kohen,* is related to the word *quarab* which means to "draw near." The priest is one who draws near to God and longs for the Lord as a deer longs for water (Psalm 42:1). As we draw near to God, He refreshes us (John 4:14) and transforms us (Romans 12:2) as worshipers who will proclaim His praises through a lifestyle that represents His Holy and loving character.

This is the bottom line of our mediatoral role as priests, representing Christ before men in such a way that He receives the glory. Worship teacher Gerrit Gustafson states, "A priest is also one who offers an acceptable sacrifice to God which is pleasing, and in harmony with His Spirit and in accordance with His truth." (1 Peter 2:5)[12]

There are many kinds of sacrifices pleasing to the Lord. Just a few include:

- Doing good to others - Hebrews 13:16
- Bringing justice to the poor - Amos 5:22-24
- Evangelism - Romans 15
- Humility and Brokenness - Psalm 51:17
- Righteousness - Psalm 51:19

It is part of our priestly privilege to bring sacrifices unto the Lord. But it will cost us something (See 1 Chronicles 21). David would not offer a sacrifice to the Lord which cost him nothing!

The Latin word for priest *"Pontifex"* means "bridge builder". Another dimension in serving as priests is in laying down our lives so others can cross over to a relationship with Christ. This is our greatest testimony. But bridges get stretched and get walked on, so we must be willing to lay down our lives in humility.

Remember how the Apostle Paul served the Ephesian Church in humility and with tears? (Acts 20:18-19) Consider the faithfulness of so many missionaries who have not only served in humbleness, but who have given their lives for the sake of the Gospel.

"I saw under the altar the souls of those who had been slain because of the Word of God, and the testimony they had maintained." (Revelation 6:9) Are we humble enough to be slain even in the little things and the inconvenient hassles musicians often face on the road? Are we willing to lay down our lives and be poured out, and not remind others that we are doing it? Whoever wants to be the greatest must be the least. Whoever wants to be royal must be humble. Pastor Scotty Smith once said *"We need to serve with a towel before we serve with a microphone."*

Pastor Bill Hybels calls this attitude "Descending Into Greatness", which is the title of his powerful book. I call it "the gospel of opposites" – the way up is down, we die to live, we lose to win, the last shall be first. It is the same paradox where Christ is strong in our weakness.

John Dawson challenges us to walk in the "opposite spirit" of the world. Hybels says that this descension seems totally illogical in a world that tells us to ascend to "fame, money, spotlights, power, comfort, and pleasure. Up, clearly, is the direction of greatness."[13]

But in the logic of the kingdom the real way up is down. Jesus, our High Priest, is the greatest demonstration of this logic, from His birth to His death.

This attitude and lifestyle of priestly servanthood is the mark of a Christian. When we approach our ministry from this perspective everything falls into its proper place. As James says, when we humble ourselves, God will lift us up, not necessarily to where we think we should be, but to *where He wants us to be. And it is there that we will ultimately find the fulfillment we so desperately seek, and the kingdom impact we were designed to make.*

The priestly calling upon our lives and ministries involves:

1. Drawing near to God: fellowship with God
2. Offering acceptable sacrifices to God: ministering to God
3. Being a bridge builder to God: representing God by serving and ministering to others.

With this kind of character we will see a new generation of Christian artists who are both royal priests and humble servants, representing God and ministering in the authority that comes with a life *filled with the Spirit of God!* This is keeping the Gospel in Gospel Music.

A Real Challenge

In his book *Rebuilding Your Broken World*, Gordon MacDonald gives a list of poignant questions that friends in accountability to one another might ask.[14] I've taken several of his questions and added a few of my own which might be helpful and healthy for Christian musicians to ask one another. Be honest.

1. How is your relationship with God right now?
2. Where do you find yourself resisting Him?
3. How are your times in His word?
4. Are you seeking Him more than your career?
5. Are you satisfied with where He has you now?
6. Are you anxious for anything in your life?
7. Are you frustrated over anything in your life?
8. Are you jealous of where other Christian artists are in their ministry compared to where you are?
9. Are you ministering in God's power or in your own?
10. Are your motives pure? Business ethical?
11. What is the state of your sexual perspective?
12. Tempted? Dealing with fantasies? Entertainment?
13. Do you like yourself at this point in your pilgrimage?

14. Are you trying to manipulate God, others or circumstances to get where you think you should be?
15. Would you say your life and ministry bears the mark of integrity?
16. Do you earnestly desire for God to change your heart to be more like Christ?

James tells us that healing takes place when we confess our sins to one another. (James 5:16) Confession moves us from victims to victors! It takes us from hiding to justification. It breaks down the walls we have between one another where we control what we want people to know about us. This kind of accountability should be reserved for mature trusted friends.

U.S. President Teddy Roosevelt, who was a devoted Christian, once said "a leader understands that failure is the backdoor to success."[15] Admitting failure in the context of these kind of mature accountability relationships is the first step towards success as we learn from our mistakes together. May we have the courage and honesty to seek this transforming dynamic of Christian fellowship!

Chapter Four

With Ability, Intelligence and Knowledge

By wisdom a house is built, and through understanding it is established: through knowledge it's rooms are filled with rare and beautiful treasures.
    - Proverbs 24:3

The splendor and mastery of Michelangelo's phenomenal ability as seen in the Sistene Chapel is ineffable. The awesome craftsmanship demonstrated in his statue of David adds sheer wonder to the city of Florence. The transcending cathedral spires of Western Europe or the colorful domes of St. Basil's in Red Square pay tribute to architectural genius. The rapture of Beethoven's *Ode to Joy* or the passion and precision of the Russian Ballet proves the power of great art.

Ability

Bezalel was given great ability. It was a gift from God, for great God glorifying art. Gene Edward Veith, Jr. wrote:

"The Exodus passage not only states that artistic talent is from God, but it goes on to detail the specific gifts needed by an artist... These gifts should not be thought of as some zap from Mt. Sinai which changed a bumbler with ten thumbs into an artistic genius. Bezalel no doubt was a skilled craftsman, in the normal course of things, before he received this divine commission."[1]

By simply applying the sane-estimate-of-your-capabilities test, (Romans 12:3) we will cognitively know if we are called to ministry through the arts.

Not everyone can sing, act, write, or paint. These are aptitudes, gifts, and talents given by God. I don't believe God would raise up a music ministry in which there was a real lack of musical aptitude, or the ability to perform and communicate through music. Can you imagine a Christian Milli Vanilli (a group who faked their entire performance)?

Yes there are times when God uses the feeble little voice in a church choir solo to minister to his people. But this does not suggest that a career in music ministry is apropos! If that was the case, everyone in the choir would have an album, God forbid. The artisans in the Bible are described and commissioned on an entirely different level. They were literally employed by divine command. Consider the qualifications of the Temple singers.

1. They originally had to be twenty-five years old (Numbers 8:24, later lowered to twenty. Also see 1 Chronicles 23: 24)
2. They were schooled in their craft and very skilled (1 Chronicles 25:7).
3. They served an apprenticeship (1 Chronicles 25:8).
4. They were under the supervision of their fathers or the King (1 Chronicles. 25:6).
5. They were legally bound by Hebrew law (the first music contracts). (1 Chronicles 15:20-21)

Artistic ability was taken very seriously. It has been said that there is bad "good music" and there is good "bad music." We are striving for good "good music." This is what the temple singers strived for. Assuming that we have talent, what are the next steps?

Intelligence

Gene Edward Veith, Jr. goes on to say that "a person may have talent, but that alone is not enough for great or God-pleasing art. God gave Bezalel a measure of understanding, of reason, of common sense."[2]

The statue of David carved by Michaelangelo is designed and balanced in such a way that it will not fall over.

The choreographers of the Russian Ballet calculate every move with meticulous detail and precision. Imagine a slight miscalculation sending a dancer spinning right off the stage. Sculpture involves the dynamics of perspective and balance. Dance involves mathematics. Both incorporate these into aesthetics. It all works together.

Intelligence comes into view for the Christian musician in such areas as understanding intonation, harmonic progression, tempo and groove. For the songwriter there needs to be an understanding of hooks, prosody, form, and use of imagery. For the sound engineer there needs to be an understanding of acoustics, equalization (and impatient artists!). For the artist, even if there is the raw talent to sing there must be an accompanying degree of how to perform or deliver. Behind all of this is the gift of knowledge.

Knowledge

Again Veith says:

"Whereas intelligence involves the faculties of the mind, knowledge involves the content of the mind. Bezalel, in addition to talent and mental acuity needed to recognize and know how to prepare acacia wood. He needed to know how to cast bronze and how gold can be beaten to microscopic thinness without tearing. Besides knowing his materi-

als, he had to know his subjects: both the natural –
the structure of almonds, flowers and pomegranates
– and the supernatural – appearance of the Cheru-
bim and the meaning and function of the mercy
seat."[3]

The point is well made. We need to be as affluent as
possible in the lexicon of our musical bent. As a songwriter,
I am often involved in song writing seminars and critique
sessions. I am often disappointed over the shallowness of so
many lyrics. I am amazed so many college graduates write
lyrics on a sixth grade level, both theologically and academi-
cally. A Christian producer recently told me about a song he
received in which the writer was asking Jesus to hold his life
together like jelly in a sandwich!

It is the precious atoning blood of Jesus which redeems
us (Ephesians 1:7), justifies us (Romans 5:9), sanctifies us (1
Corinthians 6:11), and promises us an eternal inheritance
(Hebrews 9:15). This is what holds our lives together! Yet
often in our theological poverty and immaturity we end up
contextualizing the power of the Gospel right out of the
Gospel. In trying so hard to relate to the world, we embrace
an attitude of "total fluidity." This is a missionary term used
to describe a situation where missionaries try to pour the
culture into the Gospel rather than pouring the Gospel into
the culture.

> *We need to combine Biblical fidelity with cultural sensitivity, being relevant to the world without compromising the integrity of scripture.*

Good theology leads to good communication. When I
speak of good theology I am speaking of how well we under-

stand God's word and classical Christian doctrine, and how well we apply it in our lives and ministries. Good theology leads to good discipline, good discernment, good worship, good warfare, good evangelism, and good art!

Good Discipline

In the Old Testament, when Moses was teaching Israel the decrees and commandments of the Lord, he said, "Observe them carefully, for this will show your wisdom and understanding to the nations, who will hear about all these decrees and say "surely this great nation is a wise and understanding people." (Deuteronomy 4:6)

In the New Testament, when Paul was teaching the Christians in Colossae he said, "Let the word of Christ dwell in you richly as you teach and admonish one another with all wisdom and as you sing psalms, hymns and spiritual songs." (Colossians 3:16)

And when Paul addressed Timothy he said "watch your life and doctrine closely. Persevere in them, because if you do, you will save both yourself and your hearers." (1 Timothy 4:16)

All of these passages point to discipline. Several words stand out such as **Observe carefully, dwell richly, watch** and **persevere.** All involve discipline.

The result is the nations will see God's people as wise and understanding. God's people will be able to teach and admonish each other with all wisdom and bring the truth of His salvation to those who listen. Paul's letter to the Colossians was a direct result of a strange teaching which had infiltrated the church in the form of angel worship and rigorous self denial.

In His book, *The Christian, The Arts and Truth* Frank Gaebelein talks about the "Aesthetic Imperative." His book is a powerful exhortation for Christians to regain a vision for greatness and excellency in the arts. He warns of mediocrity and ushers a clear challenge to Christians in the arts regarding their obligation to the glorious One who has gifted them.

I couldn't agree more. But in addition to an aesthetic imperative, we also need a "theological imperative". What good is great art with lousy theology? Should we have great music, great production and mediocre theological content?

King David said "Your decrees are the theme of my song" (Psalm 119:54).

I don't suggest that our music use so much theological mumbo jumbo that people cannot relate. I am saying we need to salt the pop-culture with kingdom culture. This will take devoted discipline on the part of Christian songwriters as we persevere in God's truth and then communicate that truth.

In a recent song writing class a very precious lady submitted a song to me about the death of her little daughter. Being a father of two girls myself, I was emotionally caught up in the pain of her song. But the chorus of the song suggested that her little girl now had her angel wings. I had to very sensitively remind this grieving mother that while I understood the sentiment of her song, when Christians die they are not promoted to angel status. This would actually be a demotion, because human beings are destined to judge the angels! (1 Corinthians 6:3)

We live in a culture that is obsessed with angels. Recent movies and TV shows have escalated this obsession and have introduced angels in a distorted way despite their good intentions and family appeal.

Perhaps a better understanding of Paul's struggle with the Colossian heresy would generate better songs on the afterlife. But this takes discipline as we study to show ourselves approved, as workmen who correctly handle the Word of God and relate it to contemporary culture in creative and relevant ways. Being a Greek to the Greeks and a Jew to the Jews does not necessitate compromise of truth.

"But if the salt has become tasteless, how can it be made salty again? It is no longer good for anything except to be thrown out and trampled underfoot by men" (Matthew 5:13 NASB).

In his compelling book *Are Christians Destroying America?* Tony Evans relates how salt was used in biblical days to help repair the flat rooftops of peoples homes. It was mixed with the mineral gypsum and water to a thick paste and made an excellent patching compound. In the mixing process the salt would lose its taste because of the overwhelming bitterness of the gypsum. The salt was only good then to be trampled upon as people used their roofs the way we would a porch or deck on our home.

Evans points out "That's a good description of contemporary Christianity. We've become so mixed up with the gypsum of this world's way of thinking and living that people can't taste the Christianity in the culture any more."[4]

This could also be true of our music, our message and our industry if we lose the saltiness which distinguishes us as a "wise and understanding people" (Deuteronomy 4:6). We need to "keep the Gospel in Gospel music!"

Either we are doing Christian music with the message of Christ or redemptive values, or we are watering it down so much that no one can tell the difference between our music and the music of the world.

Steve Taylor, Christian alternative rock musician, declares, "Now, having returned to the Christian music industry, I realize that what's critically important about Christian music is its distinctiveness. If it loses the cross, if it loses Christ, if it becomes just 'positive pop,'; then I'd rather be cut off from it" (CCM June '96).

I recently did an interview with Focus on the Family's *Plugged In* magazine. They raised an issue of real concern over the lyrics of some of the fringe alternative Christian "thrash" or "grunge" music that not only poorly communicates the hope of the gospel, it drags the listener into bleak, morbid and dangerous levels of existentialism and social dysfunctionalism. Titles such as "I Could Murder," "Agony," "Deceived," and "Disease" are just a few of the songs that fill these bizarre albums that rival Metallica, White Zombie, Alice in Chains or Smashing Pumpkins.

Focus on the Family compared the lyrics of these Christian groups with secular groups such as Pearl Jam and discovered that some of the secular groups had lyrics with a brighter message (*Plugged In* Oct.'96). Whoops!

One of these so-called Christian albums (found in Christian bookstores) actually offers a picture on the CD booklet cover of a person holding the skull of a beast over his head. The music sounds like the soundtrack to the Exorcist with vocal effects that resemble demonic voices amid the distorted and frantic musical sequences. The lyrics of these albums offer no redemptive hope whatsoever.

"I've got a knife that's up in the kitchen
I've got a knife that's ready to take the plunge
I've got a knife that's ready for marriage
I've got a knife that wants to have fun
I've got a life that ain't worth livin'..."[5]

"You think you're on the right path
I feel nothing but hate for you
Oh god, oh god
I could murder, I could kill"[6]

"Hate pulses straight through my veins
Every time I hear your name...
Another child scarred by your hand
Prey on those who can't defend
Forgiveness has been denied
You have left me scarified."[7]

I wonder if groups such as these are mentored by a pastor or elders who approve of this negative approach to ministry?

When one of these fringe groups appeared in Nashville, I made it a point to attend the concert. After a couple of mediocre front sets who never once said anything about the Lord, the band appeared onstage dressed in black attire with red candles burning atop amplifiers as if it were some sort of ritual.

When I confronted the band's leader and asked him where he attended church, he stated he was too busy for church. I pressed him a little further and asked him if he was accountable to anyone (pastor, elders, ministry board) who was praying for him and mentoring him. He stated he wasn't aware that this was important. It was obvious to me that his lack of understanding in this area of accountability has distorted his message and presentation.

I realize these forms of music relate to a certain disenfranchised segment of today's youth and grab their attention. But the angry and macabre lyrics lead to nowhere, despite liner notes which encourage the listener to dig for the true meaning of the songs, none of which ever mention Jesus or anything close to the hope that He brings.

Perhaps in a concert setting these peculiar songs which deal with the dark side of human emotions can be explained through personal testimony. But out there on an album, floating around, without a safe context these songs are subject to dangerous misinterpretations and consequences. The music is angry and musically dysfunctional. The message is ambivalent!

"Do not be overcome by evil, but overcome evil with good" (Romans 12:21).

Good Discernment

Michael Horton has said somewhere that "music is the incarnation of the message." I do not want to make a comprehensive statement that "music is the message" but music *most definitely* has a message (with or without lyrics).

If we just define music as a series of notes and rhythms, then perhaps it could be considered neutral. But music is a combination of notes, rhythm, words, and spirit - good or evil. Jesus said "The words I have spoken to you are spirit and they are life" (John 6:63).

Paul said that he spoke in words taught by the Spirit, expressing spiritual truths in spiritual words (1 Corinthians 2:13).

The naiveté of saying that music is amoral ignores the fact that music includes spirit. Music's spiritual element cannot be ignored. Put on a recording of your favorite praise music and you will sense an uplifting spirit that draws you closer to God.

Now put on a recording of Nirvana and listen to Kurt Cobain's "I Hate Myself and Want to Die" which he accomplished by committing suicide in April 1994. If you can't sense a different spirit representing a dejected and despondent disposition, then pinch yourself.

Without making a major case out of this controversial subject, let me just make a simple suggestion for how Christians can evaluate all art. It has been said that we should **"avoid anything which makes evil look good or good look evil."** We need to learn how to discern the spirit behind the art - even if it bears a Christian title.

A good example of discernment is found in Exodus 32. When Moses and Joshua came down from the mountain they heard the sound of singing coming from the camp of Israel. Joshua exclaimed that it was the sound of victory. But Moses more accurately discerned that it was the sound of revelry. They both heard the same sound but Moses heard the spirit behind the sound. His discernment proved right as God's people were found flagrantly dancing and singing around the golden calf they had made.

Good theology will help us better discern what it is we allow our eyes to see and our ears to hear. There is room for a million styles of music - don't build your theology on your musical taste-buds. We need to be careful not to ever put God into a box and decide for Him what He can or cannot use. But by the same stroke we need to "test the spirits" in all things to see if they are from God (1 John 4:1).

Our art needs to be real and authentic. I don't believe we should put on a fake Christian smile and gloss over the harsh realities of life, but neither should we leave people with a picture of hopelessness. The Gospel *does* mean good news, and how beautiful are the feet of them that bring that good news! (Romans 10:15) If the spirit behind the music leaves a sense of only bad news – you better check it out.

A lot of concern is raised over whether or not Christian artists should cross over to the world. ***I am more concerned about the world crossing over to Christian artists.***

> *When Christian artists cross over, the object is to "take the cross over" and to be a light in the darkness.*

As in any vocation, Christians are called to infiltrate the world as salt and light, without compromising their faith. This is just as much true for musicians as it is with doctors, lawyers and teachers. We are to take the Gospel to the world not only through the words of our mouths but through the witness of our lives. What concerns me is when the world tries to infiltrate the church.

Unfortunately the world has had more influence on Christian music than Christian music has had on the world. This is another reason why I am so convinced that all Christian artists need to be accountable to a local church, whether they are rap, pop, alternative, metal, praise or hillbilly. This is not only good discipline, it is wisdom.

Good Worship

God is seeking those who will not only worship Him in Spirit, but also in truth. (John 4:23)

Good theology leads to good worship. What we should garnish from scripture should move us from man-centered worship to God-centered worship. The scriptures alone authoritatively speak to what is acceptable worship whether by

1. precept – explicit teaching
2. precedent – example
3. principle – to worship in spirit and in truth

This axiom should also be applied to all our art. This is not restricting our freedom of expression, rather it is unleashing expression for the beauty and glory of God. Bezalel's Tabernacle account is a biblical precedent for this kind of expression.

The Bible gives us precepts about how we are to bring glory to God's name. There may not be "perfect worship this side of heaven, but there is appropriate worship," as Pastor Scotty Smith once said. Appropriate worship involves a lifestyle of worship. For example, we are told by Jesus not to offer our gift at the alter until we are reconciled with our brother (Matthew 5:23-24). We are also told to offer our lives as living sacrifices, holy and pleasing to God, which is our spiritual worship. (Romans 12:1) In over two hundred verses we are explicitly commanded to sing, to clap our hands, dance, shout, and bow before the Lord.

We are to worship in Spirit and in Truth.

The opposite of Spirit is flesh. We are not to worship in the flesh.

"These people honor me with their lips, but their hearts are far from me." (Matthew 15:8)

The opposite of truth is falsehood. We are not to worship in falsehood.

"They worship me in vain, their teachings are but rules from men." (Matthew 15:9)

How do we know the difference between the teachings of God and the teachings of men? By studying the truth. The F.B.I. experts who track down counterfeit money operations can spot a counterfeit bill very quickly because they have studied, exhaustively the real thing. Good theology leads to good doxology which leads to devotion. In his book *Desiring God*, John Piper states "The fuel of worship is a true vision of the greatness of God"[5]

Magnifying the Lord is bringing into clear close focus the awesomeness of God. It is seeing every wonder of His majesty and proclaiming it. The Greek word for worship used most frequently is *proskuneo* which means to kiss forward. Imagine bowing before a great king and leaning forward to bestow a kiss upon him. This is the picture of worship. You cannot kiss someone from afar. A kiss is intimate. It is up close and personal. You can be most honest with someone you love.

This also is worshiping in truth. King David's most revealing song to the Lord is Psalm 51 after Nathan the prophet rebuked him for his adultery with Bathsheba. David brings his broken and contrite heart before the Lord in honesty and humility. Worship is our response to God's saving grace. If we don't understand the theology of grace we will never enter into whole-hearted worship.

We learn true worship in the context of awareness of our immense need for grace and a revelation of God's intrinsic worth. If we are wrong about the object of our worship, then every aspect of our worship will be deficient, if not idolatrous! In fact, A.W. Tozer has said that a false image of God is the worst idolatry!

Good Warfare

It has been said that David stunned Goliath with a stone but slew him with a sword.

> "May the praise of God be in their mouths and a double-edged sword in their hands, to inflict vengeance on the nations and punishment on the peoples, to bind their kings with fetters, their nobles with shackles of iron, to carry out the sentence written against them. This is the glory of all his saints" (Psalm 149:6-9).

Remember when King David chose the musicians and singers along with the "commanders of the army?" (1 Chronicles 25:1) This is significant because spiritual warfare surrounds Christian music and worship.

Brothers and sisters, this is a real battle, "not against flesh and blood but against the rulers, against the authorities, against the powers of this dark world and against the spiritual forces of evil in the heavenly realms" (Ephesians 6:12).

I have wrestled against these powers in many nations around the world. From secret concerts in the former Soviet Union and the East Bloc nations to concert outreaches in Islamic West Africa and Southeast Asia. Putting on the full armor of God and wielding that double-edged sword (Ephesians 6:17; Hebrews 4:12) has been essential to the impact of my ministry around the world. I have been followed by the K.G.B., had rocks thrown at me in Africa, a gun pointed in my face on several occasions at border crossings, and had valuable equipment confiscated. At one concert in the North Western U.S. satanic priests walked back and forth in the rear of the auditorium praying against my altar call. In another concert in Africa, Muslim clerics threatened the safety of my worship team.

It is a real battlefield out there, and you don't need to go much further than your church door to find it.

The praise of God must be in our mouths and the double-edged sword must also be in our hands.

> "For the Word of God is living and active. Sharper than any double-edged sword, it penetrates even to dividing soul and spirit, joints and marrow; it judges the thoughts and attitudes of the heart" (Hebrews 4:12).

When Satan tried to tempt Jesus in the wilderness, Jesus fought back with scripture. As we face temptations as Christian artists, we will need to fight back with God's sword of the Spirit. During a missions trip to Cuba, we faced constant breakdowns of sound equipment. Immediately the Cuban brothers and sisters broke out into praise warfare.

"I will call upon the Lord,
Who is worthy to be praised.
So shall I be saved from my enemies."

They were singing out the words of Psalm 18, one of the Hebrew battle songs. The Hebrew word for praise here is *halal*, the root word for "hallelujah"! It means to shine, to boast, make a show, to rave, celebrate and be uproariously foolish.

But these precious Christians were not being foolish for praising God. They were waging warfare against the enemy by singing God's word.

* When the singers went before the outnumbered army of Israel under Jehoshaphat and sang God's praises, it threw the three enemy armies into so much confusion they began to fight each other until they were all killed. Israel was untouched (2 Chronicles 20).

* When Paul and Silas were in prison they sang hymns of praise to God. There was a violent earthquake that shook the very foundations. The prison doors flew open and every prisoner's chains came loose. (Acts 16:25) "Every stroke the Lord lays on them (his enemies) with his punishing rod (His word) will be to the music of tambourines and harps, as He fights them in battle with the blows of His arm" (Isaiah 30:32).

What a powerful combination: God's word and God's music waging warfare against the enemy. Praise silences the foe and the avenger (Psalm.8:2) In worship, lies are exposed as truth is presented. Good theology leads to victorious combat!

Good Evangelism

Where there is a high view of scripture there will be a high view of evangelism. John Stott states:

"Without the Bible world evangelization would be not only impossible but actually inconceivable. It is the Bible that lays upon us the responsibility to evangelize the world, gives us a gospel to proclaim, tells us how to proclaim it, and promises us that it is God's power for salvation to every believer. It is moreover, an observable fact of history, both past and contemporary, that the degree of the church's commitment to world evangelization is commensurate with the degree of it's conviction about the authority of the Bible. Whenever Christians lose their confidence in the Bible, they also lose their zeal for evangelism. Conversely, whenever they are convinced about the Bible, then they are determined about evangelism."[6]

In a later chapter we will look more closely at the marriage between music and missions. But John Stott is so correct in his assessment of our biblical convictions towards evangelism.

Good theology leaves no room for doubt that evangelism is at the very heart of God. It is not an option but a biblical mandate! In fact every mention of the "filling of the Spirit" in the book of Acts is in the context of evangelism. God's heart for the nations permeates scripture. The Bible gives us the mandate, the message, the model and the power!

Good Art
Rare and Beautiful Treasures

"By wisdom a house (or ministry) is built, and through understanding it is established; through knowledge it's rooms are filled with rare and beautiful treasures" (Proverbs 24:3-4, clarification added).

Solomon said that wisdom begins with the fear of the Lord and that knowledge of the Holy one is understanding (Proverbs 9:10). These build a ministry and fill our lives and our craft with rare and beautiful treasures. These are the eternal gifts we offer which plow deeper, take root, and produce fruit much greater than fleeting aesthetic pleasures. Great art is life-giving art. It is ministry. It is always nice to hear someone complement my music. But I take great delight when someone shares with me a testimony of how the Lord used one of my songs to bring direction, conviction, comfort or healing in their life.

This life giving potential adds a greater dimension and responsibility to our music. God's word doesn't return void

(Isaiah 55:11), and "is useful for teaching, rebuking, correcting and training in righteousness, so that the man of God may be thoroughly equipped for every good work" as Paul taught Timothy (2 Timothy 3:16,17). Earlier, Paul urges him to continue in what he has learned and to persevere in doctrine.

In his first letter to the Corinthians, Paul speaks of a fire that would test the quality of men's works. It is a picture of what will endure and what will fade. The contrast is between "gold, silver and precious stones" and "wood, hay and straw" (1 Corinthians 3).

This contrast is a clear picture of "**works of the Spirit**" versus "**works of the flesh**." I don't need to tell the story of the Three Little Pigs for you to figure out whether wood, hay and straw will survive the ordeal. Obviously the point is made that we should strive to build the church with lasting things - precious stones or quite literally - living stones (1 Peter 2:5). This means people! This means ministry! And this is what distinguishes Christian artists from other artists. This is the impetus for great art!

It boggles my mind when I hear of Christian artists calling themselves "legends" or referring to their songs as "classics." What we call "contemporary Christian music" is little more than thirty years old!

Martin Luther, Charles Wesley and J.S. Bach are "legends." Their songs are the "classics." If our works stand the test of time, and hundreds of years later still appear in the hymnal, perhaps then we will be legends. This is the kind of art we should strive for – not the paintings that hang on the wall of a Holiday Inn but in the corridors of the great galleries; not the songs that spend a week or two on the CCM charts, but in the hymnals of our great grandchildren. Not the trendy little toothpick lyrics of the Buckeroo generation, but the double-edged sword of God's word rendered with ability, intelligence and knowledge, all for God's glory and the **building of His church**.

Redemptive Art

I am not trying to force our art or our music into a religious corner. I believe we can express God's truths and reflect His glory before men in a way that is not "religiously overbearing." What we create should reflect a biblical Christian world view.

Much of what Bezalel created in building the tabernacle was purely for beauty and glory. It was not art for art's sake, because it was rooted in the context of relationship with God and His creation. It reflected God's beauty and God's glory just as powerfully as a golden sunset or snow-capped mountain. How far can we go in our art?

Whatever is true, noble, right, pure, lovely, admirable, excellent and praiseworthy-create these things and let God receive the glory! (Philippians 4:8 author's paraphrase).

This is what I call "Redemptive Art." It is art or music that affirms (by Spirit and truth) things which point to God and to biblical principles and solutions. While not necessarily appearing as "religious" this approach keeps the gospel in gospel music.

Songwriters and artists such as Paul Overstreet and Gary Chapman are masters of such songs which reflect the realities of life and point to biblical truth while not using "Christianese."

Bob Carlisle's "Butterfly Kisses," Bruce Carroll's "Sometimes Miracles Hide" and Bob Bennett's "Baseball" are wonderful examples of what I would call "Redemptive Art."

Harold Best in his book *Music Through the Eyes of Faith* says:

> First, all truth is God's truth even when God or
> Christ or salvation are not particularly mentioned
> in wholesome lyrics. It makes every bit of sense for
> a Christian artist to sing of love, justice, friendship,

family, parades, pain, hurt, abuse, playfulness, children, games, brotherly and sisterly love, and any number of other conditions, as long as they are driven by the same conscience and care that drive straight-ahead Christian lyrics....Second, many CCM artists have come to realize that as long as they limit themselves to playing only in "Christian" contexts, CCM, instead of reaching non-Christians, repeats itself to Christians for whom it is not much more than spiritualized background music - a kind of holy wallpaper decorating their days.[10]

Later on I will discuss how redemptive music and art play a major role in "nation-building" and reshaping or re-forming distortions of God's truths in world cultures.

Chapter Five

With All Craftsmanship
and Able to Teach

Leaders have mentors. They are disciples.
They comprehend the notion of legacy.
Theodore Roosevelt

Gene Edwards Veith says, "In addition to talent, intelligence, and knowledge, an artist needs craftsmanship; the mastery of technique. Craftsmanship involves skill at working with one's medium, whether words or paint or stone, causing that medium to do one's bidding."[1]

It is possible for someone to have ability but not intelligence or common sense in how to manifest their talent. For example, someone may be a tremendous drummer when playing alone, but not able to carry the band along with a good solid tempo. Or there might be a person who has a powerful voice yet no sense of pitch. Talent, intelligence and knowledge all work together in craftsmanship. Right brain and left brain work together in craftsmanship. Bezalel understood the nature of flowers, had the talent or ability to design and carve out flowers, and the inspiration to do it for God's glory.

In 1 Chronicles Chapter 15 David's song leader Chenaniah is described as being the "music master" or as "skillful." The Hebrew meaning behind this description is that Chenaniah was:

1. The Master of the Song
2. The Prince of Bearing the Burden[2]

There was a tremendous responsibility on Chenaniah's shoulders as he oversaw about 4,000 choir leaders, singers and instrumentalists. The term "prince of bearing the burden" comes from the Hebrew phrase *hasar hammasa* which is used throughout scripture in connection with the same burden prophets bear (Nahum 1:1; Habakkuk 1:1; Malachi 1:1).

"The word describes the whole function of the Levitical Psalm-singers as bearing the responsibility not only of singing but as also bearing the prophetic burden of speaking the prophetic word of the Lord as birthed in the singing of praise and adoration to God. The Levitical musicians were called "seers" or even "prophets". The Chronicler uses the same Hebrew term, Nibba, as an official title for the Levitical singers (1 Chronicles. 25:1) as was used for the prophets. The prophetic unction of the singers caused them to compose Psalms to be sung as did Asaph, Heman and others which were included in the Old Testament Psalms."[3]

The Prophetic Role of Music

All throughout the Old Testament there is a strong correlation between prophecy and music. Many of the Psalms contain specific references to the life, death and resurrection of Jesus.

Psalm 2:7 is a declaration of Christ's redemptive sonship (Hebrews 1:5).

Psalm 110:4 declares Christ as our high Priest (Hebrews 5:6).

Psalm 41:9 prophesies Christ will be betrayed by a friend (Luke 22:47, 48).

Psalm 22:18 prophesies that soldiers will gamble for His coat (Matthew 27:35, 36).

Psalm 16:10 and 49:15 prophesy the resurrection (Mark 16:6, 7).

Psalm 68:18 prophesies Christ's ascension to God's right hand (1 Corinthians 15:4, Ephesians 4:8).

Other psalms are used as the very music of heaven. Even the first song of the Bible, The Song of Moses (Exodus 15) is resounded in the heavenlies (Revelation 15:3, 4). The Old Covenant musicians were assembled to prophecy.

"David, together with the commanders of the army, set apart some of the sons of Asaph, Heman and Jeduthun for the ministry of prophesying accompanied by harps, lyres and cymbals" (1 Chronicles 25). The musicians were prophesying and playing as King Saul met them and received God's anointing (1 Samuel 10:5, 6).

Not only was music used in foretelling but also in forthtelling the Word of God. The Lord uses music to awaken the senses and pierce a calloused heart. He uses music to bring conviction and challenge to a complacent heart. He uses music to minister healing to a broken heart. And He uses music to rally His saints for action with united hearts. Moses used the trumpet to call God's people and the elders together. He also used the trumpet to sound the battle cry or to announce days of joy, offering, sacrifice, fasting or the beginning of a new season (Numbers 10).

"Blow a trumpet in Zion and sound the alarm in His holy mountain, let all of the inhabitants of the land tremble, for the day of the Lord is coming" (Joel 2:1 NASB).

Prophetic music does not add extra-biblical revelation. The biblical canon is closed. It alone is complete, efficacious, sufficient, inerrant, infallible and authoritative! (*Sola Scriptura*)

Rather, prophetic music **boldly** draws attention to biblical precedent and speaks **insightfully** to issues concerning the church. The prophetic gifts mentioned in the New Testament (Romans 12:6; 1 Corinthians 12:10) primarily deal with declaration, not revelation and "speaks to men for edification and exhortation and comfort" (1 Corinthians 14:3). Prophetic music proclaims "already revealed truth."

The late Keith Green spoke forth with boldness against complacency in the church. Steve Camp's music deals passionately with tough issues confronting the church, and exhorts us to live holy lives before the Lord and the world. Prophetic music is not always easy to listen to because it sounds the alarm in our hearts to wake up because we are "asleep in the light" as Keith Green sang. But whether it's a message of rebuke or comfort, it must be a clear, distinguishable sound.

> "Even in the case of lifeless things that make sounds, such as the flute or harp, how will anyone know what tune is being played unless there is a distinction in the notes? Again, if the trumpet does not sound a clear call, who will get ready for battle?" (1 Corinthians 14:7, 8).

> In prophetic singing let us heed the words of Isaiah
> "Shout it aloud, do not hold back.
> Raise your voice like a trumpet" (Isaiah 58:1).

The Power of All Craftsmanship

What a privilege, as Christian musicians, to sound a loud and clear call to the world and church today. What a responsibility to bear the title "Nibba" as the prophets did. This is real Christian music, not commercialized industry fluff. It is music on the cutting edge of eternity. But this breed of musician must hear a higher call. He must be willing to submit himself to the rigors of spiritual and artistic discipline. This kind of balance is the formula for powerful ministry.

The music which flowed from God's temple became famous outside of Israel because of it's greatness. The musicians aimed for perfection and mastery of their craft, and this peaked at the dedication of Solomon's Temple.

"The chronicler states in 1 Chronicles 5:12-13 that the singers sang and the musicians played on instruments 'as one.' This phrase in the Hebrew is placed first in the emphatic position, thus laying stress particularly on the 'oneness,' the precision and artistic excellence of their music."[4]

The worship was so powerful the priests could not even stand to minister as God's Shechinah glory filled the Temple in a cloud. This was because the dynamics of ability, intelligence and knowledge were all working together in "all craftsmanship" within the context of God inspired, God centered, and God led worship!

Consider the dynamics of King David's "press release."

When King Saul was troubled by a distressing spirit, he called upon his servants to find a skilled harp player who could ease his weary soul.

"Then one of the young men answered and said, 'Behold I have seen a son of Jesse the Bethlehemite who is a skillful musician, a mighty man of valor, a warrior, one prudent in speech, and a handsome man; and the Lord is with him" (1 Samuel 16:18 NASB).

The servant was answering Saul's cry for a **skilled musician,** yet he went on to say there was so much more to this simple harp player. Obviously skill opened the door, but his character and intelligence allowed him to stay and minister inside the house.

A mighty man of valor means courage, fortitude, resolution and tenacity. These qualities were worked into David's life as a shepherd. It takes this kind of devotion to handle stubborn sheep, to protect them from disease, parasites, wild animals, and their own deadly rampages into dangerous pastures and rushing waters. As a good shepherd David saw that his sheep were well taken care of with the best grazing and pasturage possible, where clean water ran so gently it appeared to be still.

Being a shepherd was a full time job, all through the day and night, giving his life for the sheep. It took courage and resolution to be a shepherd, and later on, David's twenty third Psalm would reflect the Lord as his shepherd. Before David would serve in the palace, he would serve on a lonely hill outside Bethlehem. Surely it was there, that his skill as a warrior was perfected as David constantly fought off the ravages of vicious predators. As the sheep pass through the valley of the shadow of death to reach the cool summer highlands, the shepherd goes before them, faithfully carrying his rod and staff (and sling shot).

David was **prudent in speech**. He was not only a gifted musician, but a gifted poet. He had great insight into the Lord, because he sought after God's own heart. Because of this, David could exercise sound judgement in practical matters. He had good common sense, was cautious in his words and demonstrated foresight in spiritual matters. David was **handsome.** What made him attractive was all of these attributes empowered by the fact that **the Lord was with him.** That was the bottom line; **God's presence**!

Just as Bezalel was filled with the Spirit of God, David was the consummate artist, shepherd and king. His reign was a foreshadow of Christ's perfect kingdom to come. What a press release that was! How I pray that God will instill this kind of skill and character in our lives and ministries with all craftsmanship!

Inspired Him to Teach

There's an old saying "Those who can't,... teach" which presupposes that those who teach are not endowed with the real talent and thus have settled for the lessor calling of teaching.

Perhaps then we should discount Plato who taught Aristotle or Paul who taught Timothy or William Kirkpatrick who mentored C.S. Lewis.

Bezalel was not only empowered to teach but "inspired" to teach. The New American Standard Version renders that the Lord "also has put in his *heart* to teach, both he and Oholiab" (Exodus 35:34).

Gene Edward Veith, Jr. states that teaching is "the time-honored relationship of master and apprentice, teaching is by God's design part of the artistic vocation"[5] God's word says "Teach and admonish one another..." (Colossians 3:16) which is directed to all Christians.

We are called to teach the nations everything that God has commanded us. (Matthew 28:20) This is called discipleship. It is a noble calling. Jesus sends us forth to disciple others to reproduce in them what God has done in us. The Christian music scene needs strong discipleship models such as the Paul-Timothy model.

This is one reason I enjoy teaching at the Christian Artists' Seminars around the world. But this is only a very small measure of what I am talking about. Praise the Lord for artists such as Michael Card, Charlie Peacock, and John Fischer who have taken musicians under their wing to mentor them artistically and spiritually. Thank God for "Musicianaries" such as Karen Lafferty who gave up a career in the limelight to mobilize and train Christian musicians for world missions! As I travel around the world I meet so many musicians who have been discipled by Karen's ministry "Musicians for Missions" under the Youth With A Mission banner. I believe that Karen has touched more lives in this way than she ever could have if she held onto her career with Maranatha Music. (Karen wrote the praise song "Seek Ye First.")

The Word talks about one chasing a thousand, yet two putting ten thousand to flight in God's power (Deut. 32:30). Who is your teacher? Who are your disciples? In the positive sense, who are you putting to flight? All through the Old Testament are examples of musicians discipling musicians (see 1 Chronicles 15 and 16; Nehemiah 11-18).

In the book of Nehemiah the musicians actually lived together in a community called The Valley of the Craftsmen (Nehemiah 11:35) and in villages for the singers (Nehemiah 12:27-29). While I am not suggesting that you move in with your favorite Christian artist, it is important for you to be in fellowship with other musicians, especially those who are willing to mentor you.

We have a Christian artist's fellowship here in the Nashville area which meets for worship, prayer and teaching. It's not a place to look for a "deal", but rather a support group. Our ultimate accountability should be to local church, but this fellowship understands the artists mindset and language in a fuller way since we are all artists. The Foundry is another ministry in Nashville which offers classes in the arts and ministry. Outreach projects and retreats are offered in addition to the classes. Gospel artist Babbie Mason hosts a songwriting seminar every spring in Atlanta. This is a scaled down version of The Christian Artists' Seminar with a more intimate atmosphere.

During the first week in August every year is the huge Christian Artist's seminar held in Estes Park, Colorado. Several hundred classes and workshops are taught by professionals in everything from songwriting to dance to drama to how to make and promote a custom album. Each evening concludes with a concert featuring many well known Christian artists. Similar seminars take place in Holland, South Africa and Asia.

The Christian Broadcasting Network (CBN) in Virginia Beach has offered a "Success in Christian Music" seminar and each Spring the Gospel Music Association offers different workshops during GMA week (Dove Awards) in Nashville. The International Christian Arts Center, in Nashville in conjunction with Artist's in Christian Testimony (ACT) the Worship and Arts Track of the A.D. 2000 and Beyond Movement and I Care Ministries (International Christian Artists Reaching the Earth) are networking Christian musicians from all around the world via the Internet.

ACT President and Founder Byron Spradlin says "Networking is one of the greatest needs facing Christian artists today-whether around their own region or around the world It is critical for Christian artists to link together if they at all hope to have the VALUE of their ministry impact clearly seen; for several reasons:

1. Validation – Often the only validation a Christian artist receives is the validation that comes from other Christian artists.
2. Affirmation – Much ministry happens alone, under the critical eye of Christian leaders out of touch with how to communicate Christian truth to a non-Christian market place, or outside of the contexts many Christians perceive as important. Therefore affirmation from Christian artist peers is critical.
3. Learning – Christian artists must keep on learning much besides their artistic craft, including the Word of God, spiritual formation, philosophy of ministry, discipleship skills, and development as servant leaders and change agents. These aspects of maturity only come through networking and relationships with others struggling with the same challenges.

4. Unity – Right here, take note that there exists a difference in union versus unity. I'm speaking not of union in organization, but rather, unity in spirit, in heart, in vision; and then sometimes, in projects.
   Coalition is key if we are going to see the Gospel communicated and our cultures impacted and, at the same time, bring along the leadership from the Churches, Mission Boards, and Academic institutions.
5. Empowerment – Hope brings power to enthuse, to endure, and to endeavor. Networking and relationships with other Christian artists are key if we are to find regular rekindling of biblical vision, values, and vantage point, not to mention enablement to move forward.

As Christian artists link together they will see an increased—even synergized—ability to serve other Christian artists and the Church around the world for the causes of Christ. Remember: its only as we serve, encourage, resource, validate and empower (S.E.R.V.E.) other Christian artists and the Church, that we move more deeply into servant leadership and the ministry to which the Lord has called us.

Addresses for these organizations can be found in the appendix of this book.

Get excited! There are plenty of opportunities for you to sharpen your skills, deepen your commitment, and catch a bigger vision of what God is doing through the arts. And then you can pass it on to all those whose hearts have been stirred to come and do the work! (Exodus 36:2).

Bezalel: A Final Note

The Gospel has been written about, sung about, painted, sculptured, danced and preached in every conceivable and creative way. But what it needs most is to be demonstrated!

The greatest work of art is the creative work the master artist does in our lives. And the greatest work of art we can offer back to Him is a reflection of His own glory through our lives. This I believe was Bezalel's heart. A man *called by name, filled with the Spirit of God, filled with ability, intelligence, knowledge and all craftsmanship with a heart inspired to teach*. The name Bezalel literally means *"In the shadow of God"* – a man who had enough character to never step out of that shadow and compete with God for his own glory.

> "How precious is thy loving kindness, O God!
> And the children of men take refuge in the shadow of thy wings.
> They drink their fill of the abundance of thy house; and thou dost give them to drink of the river of thy delights.
> For with thee is the fountain of life;
> In Thy light we see light" (Psalm 36:7-9).

Chapter Six

Six Ways to Kill Our Art

When art supplants God, it's creator, the nature of art itself is distorted.
   - Gene Edward Veith, Jr.

After the death of Solomon the spiritual pulse of Israel was like an accordion. Divided into two kingdoms, the northern and southern kingdoms were ruled separately by a succession of kings who were evil for the most part. The glorious music and worship that once flowed from the temple had diminished to a faint whisper. Only when a good king reigned and people's hearts were turned towards God did the worship crescendo. But these were rare moments and primarily in the southern kingdom.

One of these rare moments was under the reign of King Hezekiah (715-695 B.C.). The wind of revival swept through Judah and the musicians took their responsible places in the worship flow. Hezekiah imposed a special tax upon the people to help provide for the temple musicians. At one point so many gifts were brought to the temple for the musicians that special storage areas had to be built (2 Chronicles 31). God's people saw the great importance of temple worship and music was integral to its flow.

Earlier, during the time of the prophet Amos (793-740 B.C.), the deeply reverent psalm singing had reached an all time low. Because of the complacency and sinfulness of the people, the Temple worship had become empty ritual. Amos lamented over this. Although he ministered primarily to the northern kingdom, his heart also cried out to Judah in the south. The northern kingdom of Israel was enjoying a period of great wealth and a false security because of the temporary weakness of enemy nations. Social injustice and sexual immorality was commonplace.

The southern kingdom of Judah was serving as a vassal of false gods or demons (Deuteronomy 32:17; Romans 1:22-25; 1 Corinthians 10:20). The pity of it all was that the temple service continued in a dead ritualistic way. The musicians had clearly lost their focus and confused their priorities. This was due to several reasons which are obviously very similar to what is going on today in Christian music and the church.

Complacency

People's hearts were far from God because of the prosperity of the day. The people were "at ease in Zion." Because of the military weakness of the surrounding nations of Egypt, Babylon, and Assyria, and the temporal peace between Judah and Israel, the northern Kingdom of Israel was living in a sense of false security. With tremendous pride and arrogance, Israel fancied herself as first among the nations. This led not only into an attitude of thinking they were "above sin," but also to an indolent and complacent lifestyle lavished in the luxuries of the day. Amos paints a picture of Israel's most notable persons lying on beds of ivory, eating and drinking, singing frivolously to the sound of their instruments, anointing themselves with the finest oils while not having a care in the world for God's household (Amos 6:1-6).

The church in America seems to be in a good place these days. Our borders are secure, the economy is stable, and God's people are enjoying the fruit of the American dream. But the "success obsession" is blatantly edging its way into the heart of Christian music as it has much of the entertainment industry. Concert honorariums are soaring, ticket prices escalating, artist's lifestyles increasingly more elaborate and record companies are trying to hit the ball right out of the park! Yet somehow there is a deep dissatisfaction. Something is missing.

"Consider your ways! You have sown much, but harvest little; you eat, but there is not enough to be satisfied; you drink, but there is not enough to become drunk; you put on clothing, but no one is warm enough; and he who earns, earns wages to put into a purse with holes" (Haggai 1:5-6 NASB).

In Haggai's day (520 B.C.) people were so absorbed in their own comfort, they were taking panels meant for God's temple and using them in the walls of their own houses. For fifteen years the Temple sat unfinished, until Haggai spoke out. I believe this is a picture of the state of Christian music today. Instead of building the church, "God's Spiritual temple," Christian music has become caught up in the world's success syndrome. It has become another case of "ease in Zion," while not grieving over the devastation and ruin that lies around us. Christian music has been reduced to just another way of making a good living and entertaining troops who seldom leave the fort.

Consider the statistics in world missions. It is a well known fact that ninety percent of the missions force is operating in what is called the "already reached" part of the world. This is where the church has already been planted and where there is a substantial Christian witness with the ability to carry out discipleship.

However only ten percent of the missions force is operating in the "unreached" regions of the world which represents approximately two billion people or about one third of the world's population. It doesn't take a rocket scientist to figure out that something is very unbalanced here. Why are so many missionaries concentrated in the "already reached" regions? I believe it is because they feel more comfortable, more safe, and more familiar with where they are versus an unknown frontier.

Apply this scenario to the contemporary Christian music scene. Where are most of the artists concentrating? In churches, in concert auditoriums, and in their own comfortable cultural and economic surroundings. Not that we don't need missionaries to help support church plants or musicians to serve the body, but where are the pioneers and frontiersmen who go to the unreached, the unloved and the outcasts? Who are the artists willing to stand in the gap, laying down comfortable and lavish concert settings for the real gutsy kind of ministry?

> *It has been said that stars shine brighter in the darkness.*

When God told Abraham that his descendants would be like the stars of the sky, the imagery was that of innumerable stars spread out across the twilight. Can you imagine all the stars clinging together in one spot? Unfortunately this is part of the problem of contemporary Christian music. So much of the light is shed in one place, while outside of the Christian comfort zone, darkness abounds. And while we sing to the choir from our ivory pedestals, thirty six thousand children starve to death each day and over two billion are hidden from the gospel.

Impressed by the World

"The influence of other nations had also a decaying effect on the worship of the musicians. There came a desire to copy the heathen nations in their modes of singing. Assyria and also Egypt were employing the use of vibrato in their singing which was produced by pressing the fingers on the throat...Both

Assyrian and Egyptian singers were also experimenting with vocal resonance and innovative ways to produce nasal-tone quality. This caused some of the Levitical singers to concentrate on striving for personal virtuosity rather than blending together in worship to God. The individual singer desired by his implementing of vibrato and other methods to exalt his own singing ability as an art rather than to exalt God in true worship. Jealousy and competition among the singers in virtuoso recognition brought great conflict..."[1]

Christian music today is so often impressed by the sound of the world that it follows the pop industry like a shadow. I hear more people categorizing Christian artists by whom they sound like in the secular pop market, never vice versa. I am not against being influenced by other forms of music, however I am concerned about the way Christian music bows to that influence.

The music of Israel was influenced by other nations. Temple singing and Psalm writing can be traced back to Canaanite patterns. The music of the Romans was influenced by the Greeks and later passed on to Christians in the early church. The church organ was developed from the combination of the Greek panpipes and the simple bagpipe played by shepherds in the east.

As Rome vacillated between invading other countries and being invaded by the barbarian countries of northern and western Europe, different musical influences spread out like wings across the continent. From the ancient Germanic tribe of the Goths to the ninth century Franks to the Celts of Britain the evolution of western music has been built upon influence. Today's country music finds its roots in Celtic music. Early rock 'n roll is born out of Negro-spirituals.

All forms of music have been influenced by earlier or other forms of music. We should not close our ears to the history and evolution of music, or to the current trends and styles. But neither should we be obsessed with these to the point of losing our own destiny as artists. Often, Christian labels have forced artists to embrace a certain sound. Many artists have struggled in discovering their own identity as artists. Pressure from the market place has forced some artists to record music inappropriate to their calling while others have compromised their message.

The music of the world may be musically impressive in many instances, but it is only because of God's "common gifts of grace." We can learn from it, but should never be led by it. In the end, the music of Babylon will be heard no more (Revelation 18:22). But we sing a new song that is everlasting. Let our virtuosity be in the one for whom we sing!

If we were born an original, let us not die a copy!

Temptation of Financial Gain

Originally the Levite singers received a portion of the tithes of the people of Israel (Deuteronomy 26). By the time of Ezra (450 B.C.) the singers had progressed from living on these gifts to paid employees (Ezra 6:8, 9). I do not want to enter into a debate here on "honorariums versus love offerings" for the contemporary Christian musician. This is something I believe each musician must determine, based on his own convictions.

My personal opinion is that the church needs to take a more active role in the ministry of musicians and see them as missionaries. But this is a marriage that doubtfully will ever take place because of the lack of understanding on the part of the church, and the commercial pursuits and lack of accountability on the part of the musician.

Whenever financial gain becomes the most important objective in our music ministry, then we lose the focus of God's call. There is nothing wrong with making an honest profit and sustaining our ministries and our families. It is when musicians serve money as the master, rather than use it as a servant, that we lose our way.

James Moffatt said "A man's treatment of money is the most decisive test of his character – how he makes it and how he spends it."[2]

Leslie B. Flynn stated "Money reveals where our interests lie; it can direct our attitudes; it ever exposes us to the danger of worshiping it; and it represents value. Money not only talks, it screams!"[3]

The temple singers pushed for more money and tax exemption and literally went on strike and refused to sing. In the end they won all of their demands (Nehemiah 13:10). The strike was both the result of the negligence of the people to give their tithe, and the haughtiness of the musicians who had a "no pay-no play" attitude. I actually have seen Christian artists refuse to take the stage until the cash was in their hands. If our highest call as priests is to minister unto God, then this kind of attitude among the Lord's musicians is totally off base. You see, Christian music has become such big business it is hard to imagine going back to the concept of ministering by faith. Some artists insist that this is the only right way, while others demand contractual guarantees. Either way, our hearts can be obsessed with what we will get, rather than what we will give!

Exclusivism, Pride, and Covetousness for Position

The book of Nehemiah describes the musicians as living in the valley of the craftsmen (Nehemiah 11:35) and the singers in villages they had built for themselves (Nehemiah 12:29). These communities were located in the countryside around Jerusalem. Knowing the pride and stubbornness of these musicians it may be that they were dissatisfied with the temple living quarters and opted for the more exclusive suburban neighborhoods. There was a drift between the singers and the priests. The singers demanded equal rank with the priests and wanted to wear the same sacred robes. This rivalry which lasted into the New Testament times until the destruction of the temple in 70 A.D. was recorded by the historian Josephus.[3]

Christian musicians today have often demonstrated this attitude of arrogance towards the body of Christ and it's leaders. Instead of making themselves available as servants after a concert they retreat to the protection of a dressing room. At Jesus festivals many artists hide out in the trailer area which is restricted from the audience. I can understand the need for privacy and a place to get dressed, etc. But many of these artists never come out except for an occasional autograph they might give to an adoring fan.

I do admire groups such as PETRA who make a conscious effort to meet the audience as much as circumstances allow in large civic auditoriums and festivals. As it is often logistically difficult, PETRA realizes their impact offstage as well as onstage.

When contemporary Christian music began, it was mainly in coffee-houses where the audience was face-to-face. There were no backstage hiding areas because there were no stages. The artist was on the floor like everyone else! When the music was over, the artist would hang out with the people and enter into "one on one" ministry. It was great. It was where I learned how to minister to people.

Standing on a stage fifteen feet above the people and preaching is a world apart from face-to-face ministry. Today the stages are bigger, brighter and farther away. The Christian musician is a "concert artist" and much of the intimacy is gone. The audience is too much of a hassle to deal with.

The artist is untouchable. His demands have now exceeded equality with the priest. He is higher paid, higher profiled and able to jet across the country making a shallow investment into the lives of thousands.

No wonder the prophet Amos lamented when he cried out and expressed God's anger towards the arrogance and complacency of Israel's most notable. "Away with the noise of your songs! I will not listen to the music of your harps" (Amos 5:23).

Amos was denouncing empty ritual and sacrifice without repentance. The people were offering blemished lambs at the alter. The musicians were offering praise from their lips but not their hearts. It was all a sham! To God it was just noise!

Our music is just noise to God when we lose passion for Christ and passion for serving as His priests. The Christian music industry is just noise when it loses the vision and mission it has been called to.

Compromise

A very popular Christian artist told me that his record company (a major label) was threatening to drop him if he didn't quit writing such "convicting" songs. I was told by another major label to ease up on my missions oriented music because "Christians don't buy missions!"

One executive informed me that I shouldn't do a worship album because "worship is on the way out." I told him that he had better let God know about that so He could arrange something new for all of us to do when we get to glory!

Did you ever wonder why Aaron built the golden calf? He was a man of faith, chosen and called by God (Psalm 105:26; Hebrews 5:4). He was the witness, spokesman and instrument of God's power through Moses (Exodus 4:15,16) and entrusted with the ministry of the priesthood (Exodus 28).

Yet he built perhaps the most famous idol in the history of God's people. Why? Gene Edward Vieth, Jr. states.

> "Art, unfortunately, is often the means by which man worships himself. It possesses intrinsic values which are often confused with spiritual values. The golden calf of solid gold must have been splendid to see. It must have been breathtaking as it caught the sun and later the firelight. It is little wonder that the people who experienced its beauty and mystery could confuse those feelings with the beauty and mystery of the Lord. Its beauty was more immediate and accessible than that claimed for God who veiled himself in the pillars of fire and smoke.
>
> Certain art can be awe-inspiring, mysterious, peaceful and prophetic, but these great strengths of great art can cause it to be confused with an encounter with God.
>
> This is further complicated because the primary effect of art is to bring pleasure. Art is generally pleasurable while true religion frequently is not. The splendor of the golden calf was very different from the splendor that was breaking out of Mt. Sinai and terrifying the people" (Exodus 20:18).[4]

> *We live in an age where we don't always want to hear the truth, let alone deal with it. We have often used our music as an emotional pacifier rather than a spiritual plunger.*

"For the time will come when men will not put up with sound doctrine. Instead, to suit their own desires, they will gather around them a great number of teachers to say what their **itching ears** want to hear" (2 Timothy 4:3, emphasis added).

Chuck Colson says that "if the reality of man's sin was forthrightly preached it would have a shattering effect on blissful churchgoers....Many would flee their pews never to return. And since church growth is today's supreme standard of spirituality, many pastors steer away from such confrontative subjects; so do authors who want their books bought and read. So do television preachers whose success depends on audience ratings. The result is that the message is often watered down to a palatable gospel of positive thinking which will hold the audience."[5]

Aaron made what the people wanted and then blamed them for it. "Out came this calf," he exclaimed to Moses whose anger burned within him. What Aaron did brought great sin upon the people he so desperately sought to serve. He was concerned with his own image or standing among them that he failed to give them what they really needed. In essence, he didn't care enough about them so he bowed to their pressure. He pandered to his audience and, in the process, allowed them to be corrupted, cheated, and mislead.

Often Christian artists create not what they feel led to create, but what the marketplace demands. This is called congenial art! Mere Art! Another danger in what Aaron created is that the people worshiped it. The God who had just parted the Red Sea and delivered them out of the bondage of Egypt was forsaken for a golden piece of art. The people sinfully used music to dance and sing before the calf.

Veith says "When art supplants God, it's creator, the nature of art itself is distorted. Aaron was sinning against God; he was also sinning against the arts."[6]

Even good and wonderful things can become objects of our worship. The very tools used to point to God can be used to point to themselves. Israel worshiped the Ark of the covenant rather than the God who dwelled within it. Israel worshiped the Bronze Serpent rather than the God it represented.

Audiences can worship Christian artists and their music rather than the God they sing about. A friend of mind wrote a song that says "We don't worship the worship."[7] But how easy it is to get swallowed up in the music and emotion of good worship and confuse it with God's presence. Often the very liturgy that is designed to bring God true worship, is worshiped itself. This is why Christians relentlessly argue over worship and music. It usually has nothing to do with God and everything to do with personal taste and tradition. We cling more to these outward expressions of Godly affection than we do to the one to whom our affections are rightfully due!

The emphasis has been misplaced. It is like placing the value of an alter call on what the people coming forward are about to do, rather than placing the value on what Christ has already done to make an alter call even possible!

Liturgy is an art form in and of itself. It can be beautiful and inspiring. But it can also become a stuffy and dogmatic religion which refuses to change. Christian concerts can easily slip into manipulated programs that rely more on good showmanship and staging, than on the guidance of the Holy Spirit who is always faithful to keep the focus on Jesus.

Compromise for the Christian artist is when focus on God and His truths, becomes unfocused or refocused to pander to what the marketplace of itching ears want to hear!

Ritual

"Remember the Alamo" is an old saying used to conjure up heated memories of the infamous defeat of Texan troops by the hands of the Mexicans who seized a Franciscan mission in 1836 Texas.

"Remember Waterloo" echoes the same brutal sentiment, referring to the essential British victory over Napoleon in 1815 at the Belgium village of Waterloo.

The prophet Jeremiah (626 B.C.) issued a similar chilling reminder to his own generation who were living in moral default and turning their hearts to other gods. His cry was "remember Shiloh" (Jeremiah 7:12-15).

The story of what happened at Shiloh is indeed one of the saddest epitaphs inscribed on the tombstone of ministry gone terribly awry.

Shiloh was a city located in the territory of Ephraim in the Promised Land. It served as a kind of "Jerusalem" in the days of Joshua and throughout the period of the Judges. When Joshua entered the Promised Land, he set up the tabernacle, which contained the Ark of the Covenant and the Ten Commandments, in the city of Shiloh.

It was called the "tabernacle of meeting" because here God met His people and cleansed them of sin through their sacrifices.

Psalm 78 tells us that God actually abandoned the tabernacle at Shiloh and allowed the treasured Ark of the Covenant to be captured by the enemy Philistine army.

Why would God abandon His holy meeting place?

The Ark of the Covenant was Israel's most cherished possession. It represented God's throne, God's presence, God's power and God's glory.

Whenever Israel fought the enemy nations, their confidence in battle was knowing that God was with them, dwelling within the Ark. (However this became more of a superstitious belief in the material Ark and not in the God who dwelt within it.)

The Ark represented Israel's history: the Tablets of Law, the Golden Pot of Manna and the Budding Rod of Aaron. It also foreshadowed Israel's future as it symbolized the person and ministry of Christ (Hebrews 9:1-14). Without it Israel was doomed. Yet God sovereignly allowed the Ark to be captured by the enemy and His glory departed from Israel.

This story unfolds under the time of the Aaronic priesthood when the High Priest Eli and his sons Hophni and Phinehas oversaw the responsibilities of God's temple. Eli's sons, though Priests were full of wickedness and contempt towards the holy things of God.

They inappropriately took sacrifices for themselves and turned the people's hearts away from the Lord because of their greed. They also turned the entrance of God's meeting place into a brothel (1 Samuel 2:12-25).

Even though Eli had blessed Samuel as a little boy, Samuel's first prophecy ironically announced the destruction of Eli's household. The ark of the covenant, Israel's most cherished possession, was captured by the Philistine army, and in the battle both of Eli's sons were killed.

A messenger brought news back to Eli about the death of his sons. He was grieved. But when the messenger told him that the ark had been captured, the news was too horrible for Eli to bear. He literally fell backwards off his chair, hit the gate and broke his neck and died.

The presence of God was gone and Israel lamented. Eli's daughter in law was with child.

"When she heard the news that the ark of God had been captured and that her father in law and her husband were dead, she went into labor and gave birth, but was overcome by her labor pains. As she was dying, the women attending her said "Don't despair; you have given birth to a son." but she did not respond or pay any attention. She named the boy Ichabod, saying "The glory has departed from Israel" (1 Samuel 4:19-21).

Following the deaths of Eli and his sons, the treasured Ark of God disappeared from the embrace of Israel. After only seven months, several supernatural calamities spooked the Philistines.

For several days the Philistine priests found the statue of their idol Dagon, which resembled a fish with a man's face, fallen over into a bowing position before the Ark. One morning the statue was broken into pieces. A plague of boils also fell upon the people. It was time for the Ark to go, so they built a new cart for the Ark, loaded it with a trespass offering, and hooked it up to two cows who had just given birth. The cows supernaturally left their calves behind and headed straight to the land of Judah where it came to a rest in the field of Joshua.

Even as God had brought severe judgement on the Philistines, He also brought judgement on Israel as over fifty thousand men were struck dead when they inappropriately looked into the ark on it's return. Even though the ark was back in Israel, God's glory would be withheld until the reign of King David roughly one hundred years later. (1 Sam. 7:2) From the time of Eli to the reign of David, the priesthood was basically ritualistic, religious routine.

Jumping ahead four hundred years after David, the prophet Ezekiel expressed God's anger and judgement upon those He had chosen to be His priests.

"The Levites who went far from me when Israel went astray and who wandered from me after their idols, must bear the consequences of their sin. They may serve in my sanctuary, having charge of the gates of the temple and serving in it; they may slaughter the burnt offerings and sacrifices for the people and stand before the people and serve them. But because they served them in the presence of their idols and made the house of Israel fall into sin, therefore I have sworn with uplifted hand that they must bear the consequences of their sin, declares the sovereign Lord.

They are not to come near to serve me as priests or come near any of my holy things or my most holy offerings; they must bear the shame of their detestable practices. Yet I will put them in charge of the duties of the temple and all the work that is to be done in it" (Ezekiel 44:10-14).

The picture here is clear. Perhaps even worse than death, God allowed these fallen priests to still serve in the temple. But they could not come close to God. The intimacy was broken. All that was left was cold- blooded religion with no glory. What a horrible thought to think that we can slip into a ministry of dead works. Wasn't this the reason Jesus rebuked the Pharisees?

The Pharisees had all the right credentials, all the right connections, all the right moves and all the right rhetoric, but there was no glory! On the outside they were slick, but on the inside they were dead. No wonder Jesus called them "whitewashed tombs."

> *There are two kinds of glory. The glory of man and the glory of God. Man's glory entertains. God's glory transforms.*

"Now the Lord is the Spirit, and where the Spirit of the Lord is, there is freedom. And we, who with unveiled faces all reflect the Lord's glory, are being transformed with ever-increasing glory" (2 Corinthians 3:17, 18).

The Pharisees were bent on entertaining. They were trying to impress others with their self centered song, but their music was dead. It didn't impress Jesus. He saw that it was all "just a show." And yet He allowed them to carry on in all of their religious duties. Their time would come and their sham would be exposed.

How sad when artists reduce Christian music to mere routine and formulas in the midst of all the bright lights and hippest sounds. How sad when they become so caught up in the song of self-aggrandizement that they circumvent God's glory.

This is what the sons of Eli did when they robbed God of His sacrifices.

How sad when Christian artists have to fake it in concert and muster up their enthusiasm to cover over a life defeated by sin or an empty heart because of little or no fellowship with Christ. How sad when these musicians can no longer speak with authority and must water down the ministry while going through all the motions of a good show.

Can God still use musicians in this condition? For a season God may allow those whose passion is misdirected, but eventually He will bring them to a day of accountability. Hopefully their broken and contrite heart, and true repentance will restore the value of their ministry. If sin continues, God's discipline may be more severe as in the case of the sons of Eli the High Priest. God may even allow the death of a ministry. This has happened in Christian music before, and the painful tragedy hits all of us.

We must remember that **God is more concerned with our character than He is our ministry**. Whatever He chooses to do is out of His perfect love for us.

Jim Bakker, of the PTL Club scandal, now praises God for allowing him to go to prison. He says that God literally saved his life and saved him from himself. Praise God for this kind of severe mercy which leads to wonderful restoration.

The challenge to us, as we reflect over the roller-coaster history of biblical and contemporary priests and musicians, is to examine our own hearts and motives.

Have we lost our passion for Christ and our intimacy with Him? Are we allowing Him to tabernacle (dwell) in our hearts and ministries? Or is the seduction of worldly success trying to capture the ark of His glory, power and presence?

Two Priestly Lines

Let's go back to Ezekiel's commentary for a moment. He is speaking of a line of priests who God still allows to serve Him, but only from a distance. They may not come close to His holy things. But Ezekiel goes on to talk about another, *faithful line of priests* who have a greater privilege.

> "The priests, who are Levites and descendants of Zadok and who faithfully carried out the duties of my sanctuary when the Israelites went astray from me, are to come near to minister before me" (Ezekiel 44:15).

Ezekiel goes on to say that these priests alone may enter God's sanctuary and come near to His table. So there are two lines of the Priesthood. We have just learned that the line of priests who may come close to the Lord and His holy things are the faithful priests from the line of Zadok.

The other line of priests are limited in their service to God because of previous abominations which relate all the way back to the sons of Eli.

Remember Samuel's prophecy regarding the destruction of Eli's household?

This came to a final fulfillment when Abiathar, Israel's High Priest during King David's reign, betrayed David by supporting a rebellion against him. Although Abiathar had stood faithfuly along David's side since the days of King Saul, this last act of betrayal caused him to be stripped of his most holy priviledges. This fulfilled Samuel's prophecy because Abiathar was a descendant of Eli. It put a big exclamation mark on the end of Samuel's prophecy!

A new order of priesthood was now established under Zadok the priest who stood faithfully with David until the end. This is the order of priests who may come close to God as Ezekiel explained. Zadok's name even means "Righteous."

One order of priests sold out. They were unfaithful to God, unfaithful to others, and unfaithful to the priesthood by using it for what they could get out of it for themselves. It is amazing that God still allowed them to serve, but it was all just routine stuff.

The other order of priests were able to come close to God and His holy things. Theirs was an intimate ministry, full of the power of God's anointing. All Christians are invited as God's royal priesthood to participate in an even newer order of priesthood established by Jesus, our High Priest (Hebrews 4:14).

This order, as with Zadok's, is full of life and passion. In this order devoted hearts find joy and fulfillment in ministering unto the Lord and His people. They come to Mount Zion, the heavenly Jerusalem, the city of the living God with thousands upon thousands of angels in joyful assembly (Hebrews 12:22). Why would any priest want to return to the old order? Why would any Christian musician want to exchange this kind of glory for the ritual of just a good show?

Here's a prayer for faithful priests:

Lord when I step out onto the stage of my ministry.
I want to unequivocally know that your anointing is
upon me.
I want to minister in the power of your Holy Spirit,
not in my own power.
I want to minister in the freedom of your Spirit, not
in my own formulas and routines.
I want to know your transforming, ever-increasing
glory, and intimacy with you.
I want those who listen to my songs to experience
your transforming ever-increasing glory, and intimacy with you.
And most of all, I want you to receive all the glory
and honor forever and ever, Amen.

"Therefore I do not run like a man running aimlessly; I do not fight like a man beating air. No, I beat my body and make it my slave so that after I have preached to others, I myself will not be disqualified for the prize" (1 Corinthians 9:27).

> *God has not called us to be successful.*
> *He has called us to be faithful.*

I can think of no other greater way to be successful, than to be faithful. When I step out onto the stage of my ministry, I want to unequivocally know that God's glory and anointing is upon me. Where the Spirit of the Lord is, there is freedom.

I want to minister, not out of formula and routine but out of true freedom in the Spirit. I want to reflect God's transforming, ever-increasing glory in every chord and every note of my life and my music. This is my prayer for Christian music as well. May no one ever cry "Ichabod" over us!

Chapter Seven

Music With a Mission

He is no fool who gives what he cannot keep to gain what he cannot lose.
   - Jim Eliott

"The Daliangshan mountains of central China spread before us. An unpenetrated fortress of animism, they are the home of the Yi people.

Our group drew much attention. We had been in the area for several days praying and preparing for God to break through in a mighty way.

It was 2:15 and we began to sing and praise the Lord. Malaysian, Singaporean, Chinese, Australian and American voices blended in the songs of the Kingdom of our common Christ. Power was building in our unity. We were standing on a massive set of ancient steps which led to the Historical Center of the Yi people. In front of us was a twenty foot statue of the Yi warrior. We looked over his shoulder at the mighty mountain's majesty and with each song, faith and anticipation built within us.

The crowd gathered. They were stopped in midstride as music and dance flowed forth from us. Horn and tambourine called them to halt their activities and give attention to Heaven's appointed hour.

2:40 - The police and military arrive and ask us if this is religious activity. "Not religious" we answer as we continue to sing the high praises. They join the curious crowd and actually appear to be enjoying the praise.

2:50 - Reporters from local papers and magazines arrive and begin to take pictures and tape this music so strange to their ears.

3:00 - The trumpets sound. Their hollow echo rolls on the warm day air from mountain to mountain as we declare 'Jesus is Lord' and 'Let my people go, says the Lord.'

As we shout and dance, there is a great release of faith. Such joy breaks forth that even the police rejoice. We play sustained blasts on the horns and more people come. God is moving!
We walked right through a great hole in Satan's defenses. As the weeks pass we find entire villages open to us. The police have stepped back and we are able to lead whole families to Christ. God gives us the first church in the history of the Yi people. There has never been a church and now there is!
God has honored all of us with such a great treasure. Look at a map of China. Find Sichuan Province. See Chengdu. Just below is Xichang. Go ahead, touch it. You now have family there. Go ahead, weep, rejoice, laugh, sing, for "that which was barren has now brought forth fruit!..."

As I read this gripping newsletter from my "musicianary" friend living in Asia, I thought of the words of Plato: "Give me the music of a nation, and I care not who makes its laws; I will control its people." Later in history Karl Marx spoke almost these same words.

Yet from the sound of David's harp to the majestic hymns of Martin Luther to the driving beat of Christian groups like Newsboys and D.C. Talk, God has used music to help accomplish His plan of redeeming a people for Himself from every tribe, tongue, and nation. As one Christian music historian noted – *MUSIC BRINGS REVIVAL AND REVIVAL*

BRINGS MUSIC! With 839 references to music in the Bible and 200 verses which command us to sing, our missionary God reveals His will for music and worship to walk hand in hand with world evangelization. In the Psalms, God's song book, there are 76 references to the nations.

"Awake my soul! Awake, harp and lyre! I will awaken the dawn. I will praise you, O Lord, AMONG THE NATIONS. I WILL SING OF YOU AMONG THE PEOPLES" (Psalm 57:8, 9, emphasis added).

The prophet Isaiah cries "Give thanks to the Lord, call on His name; make KNOWN AMONG THE NATIONS what He has done, and proclaim that His name is exalted. SING TO THE LORD for he has done glorious things; LET THIS BE KNOWN TO ALL THE WORLD" (Isaiah 12:4, 5, emphasis added).

When my friends sang before the Yi people in China they were literally singing before the peoples (Psalm 108:3) and before their gods (Psalm 138:1). The praise of God was in their mouths and the double-edged sword was in their hands (Psalm 149:6-9). The unseen forces controlling this land, as well as the police and soldiers were bound with fetters and retreated at the sound of God's praise!

King David certainly understood the power of God's music in evangelism. "He put a new song in my mouth, a hymn of praise to our God. Many will see and fear and put their trust in the Lord (Psalm 40:3). This is dramatically demonstrated in II Chronicles 20, when a vast army came against Jehoshaphat and God's people. The alarmed King appealed to the Lord for help on the basis of the Abrahamic Covenant: God's promise of posterity, land, and mission to His people (Genesis 12:2, 3).

The Spirit of the Lord came upon a musician, Jahaziel, who instructed Jehoshaphat that the "battle belongs to the Lord."

Jehoshaphat sent singers out ahead of the army of the Lord. As they began to praise, the Lord set ambushes against the enemy armies who were defeated by destroying each other!

The fear of God came upon *ALL THE KINGDOMS OF THE COUNTRIES* when they heard how the Lord had fought against the enemies of Israel. **EVANGELISM!**

John and Charles Wesley were known to have said that more people were won to Christ from their hymns than from their sermons. One of the greatest missionary high points of Europe was brought about through the life of John Huss (1400 A.D.) who himself was inspired by the hymns that traveled from England as the result of reformer John Wycliffe. Huss even sang a hymn as he was burned alive at the stake because of the Pope's condemnation of the great revival which took place.

Consider the revivals of the late eighteen hundreds in America. People said that the ones Moody couldn't reach with preaching, Ira Sanky (the song leader) would reach with singing. No doubt the Billy Graham crusades would not be complete without the heart warming voices of people like George Beverly Shea, Steve Green or Steven Curtis Chapman.

Paul the apostle speaks his heart in Romans 15:9-10 through the words of the psalmist "I will praise you among the Gentiles. I will sing hymns to your name...Rejoice O Gentiles, with His people...Praise the Lord, all you Gentiles, and sing praises to Him, all you peoples."

Paul's motivations was to raise up worshippers from every tribe, tongue, and nation. The new song in Revelation 5:9 is a song shared by all nations. Jesus has purchased men for God from every one of them including the Yi of central China who have recently received this wondrous news!

Thank God for music, this "great and glorious gift next to theology" as Martin Luther put it.

In a recent article, Mary Lou Totten of the Fellowship of Artists for Cultural Evangelism based at the U.S. Center for World Mission, shared about one African Mission organization that requires foreign missionaries to study the indigenous music of the tribe they will be working with before they can begin.

Having been to Africa many times, I can vouch for the wisdom of this requirement. Music and rhythm reflect the language of the African heart. Many African pastors actually preach the sermon on Sunday morning with the choir singing simultaneously.

"Music is the key to the Frenchmen's heart" I was told in a letter from a Mission to the World missionary in Paris. In the Operation Mobilization magazine *Indeed*, the front page told about a journalist in Indonesia who was imprisoned for publishing his research that showed Indonesian youth were more interested in Michael Jackson than Mohammed (Spring '92).

During a recent missionary concert tour of Japan I was told that tickets for the Madonna concert were going for $1,000 each on the black market. In Sweden the rock group ABBA grossed more than the Volvo Corporation.

Another mission group to the Muslims told me the only way into Saudi Arabia is through the military, oil business, or the entertainment industry. "Young Saudis love the American pop culture and music."

Music is such a strategic key to world evangelization because it is the *Language of the Heart*. It is the song that rallies the church to obedience to the Great Commission. It is the sound of the trumpet, the ringing of the tambourine, the clapping of hands, and the singing of God's people as we declare HIS glorious works to all peoples of the earth! It is part of the discipling of nations (Colossians 3:16), the fellowship of the saints (Ephesians 5:18), and the symphony of heaven's triumph as the great multitude which no man can number from every nation, tribe, people, and language stand before the throne and SING!

The Parable of the Tractors

Sitting in the old rocking chair on my front porch is my favorite place in the world to think, pray, and write songs. Even in the Tennessee humidity I still manage to slip out on the porch at least once a day.

The view is awesome as our house sits up on a large hill overlooking several fields and pastures of the dairy farm below. Sometimes the soothing hum of the farmers tractor adds to the emotion of the song I'm plucking out on my road-weary guitar. I can't help notice the farmer systematically plowing back and forth, row by row, patiently making his way across the field, preparing it for a new alfalfa crop for his cows to graze on come spring.

But one day two tractors each worked their way, row by row, towards the center of the field. I was glad to see my neighbor getting the help of that additional tractor, for sometimes it would take all day for one man to plow the field. As I watched the almost hypnotizing rhythm of the tractors, my mind drifted away from the song I was working on. I wondered how quickly the field could get plowed with three tractors, no, maybe five or ten or twenty tractors. What would happen if there were a few hundred tractors, all criss-crossing the same field, cutting each other off, banging into one another and racing each other down the freshly plowed rows. Obviously, too many tractors would have been chaos. As I laughed at the absurdity of this daydream, my eyes focused on the other fields and pastures nearby. No tractors, just empty fields. Can you see the picture? One field filled with a multitude of tractors kicking up the dust and almost fighting each other for turf, and then several other fields lying quietly in the autumn sun.

The Lord began to impress upon my heart that this was a picture of contemporary Christian music where all the musicians are plowing the same field. I saw it clearly: the criss-crossing, cutting each other off, banging into each other and racing for the same turf. And all the while, so many fields lay unplowed. Do you see the picture now? Ironically, later that week I found these startling words in the Book of Jeremiah.

"This is what the Lord says to the men of Judah and Jerusalem, Plow your unplowed fields! For if you don't, my anger will spread among you like a fire!" (Jer. 4:3)

Jeremiah is using this figure of speech to show the need for spiritual renewal among his own people. In a sense their hearts were neglected and untilled hearts. In the same way, this call extends beyond God's own people.

"It is too small a thing for you to be my servant to restore the tribes of Jacob and bring back those of Israel I have kept. I will also make you a light for the gentiles, That you may bring my salvation to the ends of the earth" (Isaiah 49:6).

God has called His people to be a light to the nations in addition to their ministry among one another. Remember the statistics I shared earlier? Ninety percent of the missions force is operating in the already "reached" parts of the earth. These percentages are probably similar to the ratio of Christian artists who stay within the comfort zone of their own cultural, geographical, and economical upbringing, versus those who pursue the frontiers of not only the unreached, but the forgotten nations of this earth.

Granted, there needs to be music ministry where we live, but most cities in the U.S. host Christian concerts routinely, sometimes several concerts across town from each another on the same night. The vast majority of the audience is usually Christian.

The U.S. is saturated with Christian music. In 1996 Christian music sold 538 million dollars worth of music(GMA statistics). Thousands of artists and groups gave over 2,600 concerts (listed in CCM Magazine) not including ministry at camps, conferences, and Sunday morning services. 1,500 Radio stations played thousands of Christian songs to an audience numbering in the millions. Christian television featured hundreds of artists, and the beat goes on...

How many Christian concerts or musical outreaches took place in places like Japan? Japan is not one of those mosquito infested places, but is one of the most technologically developed countries in the world. Yet less than one percent of its 127 million people are Christian.

The most popular music among the Japanese is western pop music. The country is a wide open door because of its attraction to western pop culture. Many who have attended my concerts in Japan are college students eager to learn the English language. It doesn't matter if I'm singing about Jesus or jelly beans, they just want to hear English. What a great opportunity to present the gospel!

What about India? How many Christian artists toured India last year? With over 1.3 billion people, nearly sixteen percent of the world's population, India is one of the least evangelized countries in the world according to Operation World. Less than four percent of its 4,635 people groups have a church planted within their midst. Yet India is the second largest music buying country in the world next to the United States. Most U.S. Christian music is not distributed there because the exchange rate between the rupee and the dollar is so low that very little profit can be made. But the door is open for those who don't see profit as the bottom line. Right now in India, western pop music is the rage of the younger generation. Is God trying to tell us something? Why is it that groups like Bon Jovi will tour India, while Christian bands and artists continue to plow the same field of America and other "already reached" parts of the world over and over again while not *pursuing* the "unreached"?

I hear more people using Acts 1:8 as grounds for staying in Jerusalem.

"But you will receive power when the Holy Spirit comes on you; and you will be my witnesses in Jerusalem, and in all Judea and Sumaria, and to the ends of the earth" (NIV).

Most American Christians really hang tight on the "beginning in Jerusalem" part, saying that we need to start at home in our own Jerusalem.

First of all, Jesus said "beginning at Jerusalem" which indicates that it doesn't stop at Jerusalem, but goes on to Judea, Samaria and to the rest of the world.

Secondly, Jesus addressed this commission to His disciples who were from Galilee, not Jerusalem. For the disciples, being in Jerusalem was already "cross cultural!"

So what's our problem?

> *The problem is that most Christian artists are not thinking "Kingdom," they are thinking "career." They are not thinking "mission," they are thinking "market."*

Going to many of the unreached nations in the world is not the greatest career move. Half the time you can't even sell your tapes for what you paid for them! The sound systems are of inferior quality (assuming they even have electricity) and often the hotel rooms are like something out of Indiana Jones. The water is swimming with all kinds of critters and sometimes the food...well, it makes for great stories when you get home!

"Where He leads me I will follow,
What he feeds me I will swallow!"

"Kingdom moves" require Christian musicians to think and act on an entirely different level. We must realize that God's glory among the nations is the goal, not the success of our careers.

It is when Christian artists "discover the unique contribution that they can make to advance the Kingdom, no matter how small or insignificant it may seem. Whether classical, contemporary, or cross cultural, lets take up the challenge and join the army of artists and musicians God can use until righteousness and praise will spring up before all nations." (Isaiah 61:11) says Frank Fortunato, International Music Director for Operation Mobilization.

Missions is the pursuit of God's glory and righteousness among the nations. It is an invitation to the nations of the earth to come and worship before Him.

> "let the people praise thee O God;
> let all the people praise thee!
> let the nations be glad and sing
> for joy!" (Psalm 67:3-4)

John Piper says that "worship is the goal and fuel of missions. It is the goal of the church to bring the nations into the white hot enjoyment of God's glory. The goal of missions is the gladness of the peoples in the greatness of God."

Worship is also the fuel of missions. "Passion for God in worship precedes the offer of God in preaching. But you can't commend what you don't cherish. Where passion for God is weak, zeal for missions will be weak."[1]

As I stated in the beginning of this book, our passion in contemporary Christian music has been misdirected. The reason we don't see very much cross-cultural vision or ministry in CCM is because the passion is more focused on ourselves than it is on finishing the final task Jesus commissioned us with.

Steve Camp once commented during a panel discussion "that the problem with God's army is that all the soldiers want to hang out at the fort."

How sadly true this is. We have such nice forts here in America. We have spent millions on these forts to make them as posh and as comfortable as possible. Just look at the statistics:

⟨ Out of every dollar put in the offering plate on Sunday morning approximately 96 cents stays at home. Out of that 40 cents goes to building funds!

⟨ Out of the 4 cents that makes it overseas, less than one fifth of one cent goes to reach the hidden people (the unreached where there is no church at all).

⟨ Evangelicals spend more money on pet food than on world missions!

⟨ There is one missionary for every one million Muslims!

⟨ There are more missionaries to the state of Alaska than all of North Africa above the equator.[2]

Christian musicians have such an incredible opportunity to link up with mission organizations or church missions outreaches that it is staggering!

It doesn't mean that you need to get a pith helmet and learn to speak Swahili. It doesn't mean you need to commit to a life-time in the jungles of the Amazon raising your kids as poison dart warriors.

It does mean:

1. Becoming a world Christian **thinker** by becoming aware of what is going on in the world.

2. Becoming a world Christian **prayer warrior** by praying for the nations to see God's glory.

3. Becoming a world Christian **sender** by helping others get to the mission field.

4. Becoming a world Christian **goer** by assisting mission teams or mission bases through your musical gifts.

5. Becoming a world Christian **mobilizer** by raising up a generation of world Christians through your songs and concerts.

Being obedient to the great commission is not an option. It is a mandate!

But it's really not that scary. Understanding God's purposes can take your ministry to a whole new dimension as you discover the goal is not your career. It's all about Christ's Kingdom.

The word of God tells us that without a vision the people perish, or go unrestrained. It is a picture of people wandering aimlessly while letting an opportunity slip through their fingers.

Many Christian artists wander aimlessly from one dream to the next, all the while letting great opportunities slip through their fingers.

What is your vision? What is your call?

Listen. If the Lord has gifted you and called you, He has a specific plan and purpose for you in His Kingdom. Your career is not the issue. Let God take care of that. I applaud artists like the Tavanis who have a clear cut call to urban ministry. They speak the language, they know the turf and they are surrounded by a team of Christians who hold them accountable. They are musicians with a mission and nothing stands in the way, even the temptation of the commercial hype of the industry.

Other artists such as Michael Card and Steve Fry have devoted their time to teaching, pastoring, and writing. Many unsung heroes of Christian music have literally joined organizations such as Youth with a Mission, Campus Crusade for Christ and Operation Mobilization as staff artists and worship leaders.

Praise God for "musicianaries" such as Bill Drake, Bobby Michaels, Dave Durham, Chris Christiansen and Graham Kendrick who have plowed the unplowed fields with fervor!

One of the most exciting things is seeing a ministry strategy develop for these artists, where they are not running around aimlessly, but moving forth with real purpose and passion.

They may never see their songs on the top ten or win the mighty Dove, but they will store up in heaven a precious treasure that will last for eternity. They will be the ones who go deeper rather than wider, and impact lives for the Kingdom in a far more substantial way.

They don't need a big name to minister, just a big heart for God, for others, and for the world!

Ethnomusicology

As popular as western music is around the world, we must realize no one style of music will work in every cultural context. From this standpoint, ethnomusicologists argue that music is not the universal language comprehensively.

Tom Avery states that "no matter how much a hymn, Gospel song, or praise song means to me, it will not mean the same thing to a person raised in another musical culture. It may sound sad to that person; it may sound like noise. But even if it is pleasing to their ears, it remains foreign."[3]

Tom Avery and other Christian ethnomusicologists are pursuing culturally-sensitive approaches to encourage the development of indigenous hymnody in which the local people themselves produce Christian songs in the local language and music system.

Another tremendous way Christian artists can touch the world is by helping other cultures reclaim the uniqueness of their own musical expression for the glory of the Lord. As I travel around the world I hear mostly western songs with the local translations. This is obviously much easier and less time consuming than analyzing the traditional music of each culture.

But what a joy it is to see the nations offer their own personal and unique sacrifice of praise unto the Lord! Perhaps God can use you through the wonderful ministry of ethnomusicology as you disciple the nations in their worship!

The Storytellers

Mikko hung her head in shame. The glaring eyes of the priest pierced her heart like a swift arrow. She had spoken her mind among the men without their permission. A horrified look captured every face in the room. A woman had crossed over the line and raised her voice above the men. The sharp rebuke of the priest was most certainly in order. Mikko had disgraced herself and her husband who would now have to deal with this embarrassing matter privately at home in a forceful manner.

Halfway around the world Wugomi held his tiny son in his arms for the last time. The belly of the infant had swollen up as if stung by a thousand wasps. His hair had turned a ruddish red. Wugomi cried as he swept the flies from the face of the lifeless body. But this is the way of the land. Starvation and malnutrition were just another part of the day to day existence of the Mulawi people. The elders and storytellers had passed the stories down from generation to generation. Forever hungry, forever poor, the villagers accepted their inevitable fate and Wugomi knew there was nothing he could do to break the cycle.

Meanwhile in the snow capped mountains a thousand miles from nowhere, Naopli shivered with the chilling fate which beset her. As her mother had faced the brutal consequences of the Yali tradition, Naopli knew she too would follow because of her husband's passing. Widow strangling had been around for centuries and Naopli would not pave the way for the path of reform. It was her duty to honor the tradition. And so with one last gaze at the place she called home, Naopli loosened her collar and prepared to die.

These specific stories and the people are fictitious, but the realities are frightenly true. They represent horrifying distortions of God's truth and morality. They are but a few of Satan's deceptions among world cultures. From cannibalism to infanticide, from ritual prostitution to witchcraft and sorcery, Satan deceives the nations (Revelation 13:14: 20:8-10) and holds them in bondage to the most heinous sins of human degradation. Less serious distortions, yet none the less dehumanizing include systems of caste, slavery and polygamy.

These grotesque and demonic distortions are incompatible with the Christian Gospel no matter what culture they are manifest. They are no less horrible in the sophistication of the west, which actually mirrors them in acts of abortion, patricide and sexual promiscuity, etc.

By the late 1960's Francis Schaeffer pointed out something very important related to artists and storytellers: The philosophers (and in many traditional societies, the religious leaders or shamans) put forth the world view into the society. Then the professionals and the politicians institutionalize that world view. And finally, the general population get steamrolled with that world view.

If the storyteller is, in fact, that powerful, imagine then...from a Christian's perspective...how important is the role of the Christian artist and storyteller in seeing the Christian world view spread through any given society. That artist or storyteller is able to tell the Gospel story in winsome ways that really pluck the heart strings of that society.

How Music Can Disciple the Nations

We must understand that in every culture there are four basic components that set the pace. Colin Harbinson, Director of Youth with a Mission's Academy of Performing Arts in Ontario, Canada has created a diagram which illustrates these four areas.

WORLD CULTURES

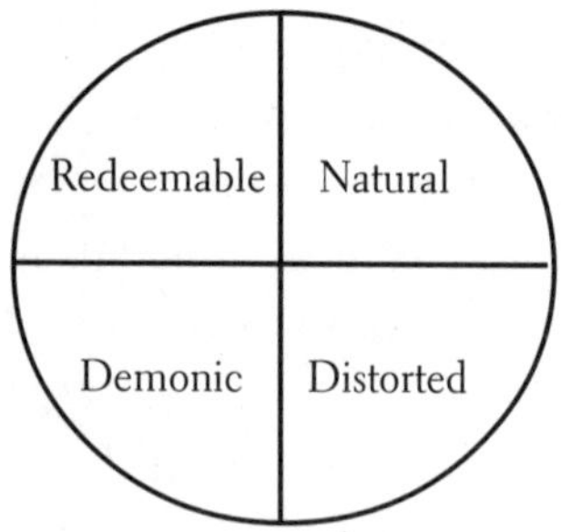

Here is a summary of Colin's diagram.

1. The **Redeemable** is that part of a culture which is "wholesome and enriching in art, science, technology, agriculture, industry, education, community development, and social welfare."[4] It is also the intuitive understanding between good and evil. For example in most cultures, murder and theft would be considered wrong. Even the cannibals described in Don Richardson's book *Peace Child* found it repulsive to eat the flesh of another man.

The apostle Paul states that God's righteous decrees have been made plain to all men and have been clearly seen (Romans 1:18-32). And this applies to all cultures whether they acknowledge God or not.

2. The **Demonic** is that part of a culture which has succumbed to "every kind of wickedness, evil, greed and depravity," (Romans 1:29) under the insidious possession of satanic forces.

It is the ultimate deception of the nations where worship of the true God is subverted by the worship of spirits, demons and the devil himself, through witchcraft, sorcery and idol worship (Deuteronomy 18:9-13). It is the spirit of anti-Christ (Deuteronomy 18:9-13).

3. The **distorted** is that part of a culture which has produced traditions or customs that pervert biblical morality and ethics such as seeing deception as a virtue or fornication as proving one's manhood or widow strangling as a means of assuring that husbands will not enter the next world unattended when they die. The "distorted" covers a wide extreme of customs, traditions, ethics, morality, philosophy and religion. "Their thinking becomes futile and their foolish hearts darkened" (Romans 1:21).

4. The **natural** is that part of a culture that expresses the God-given uniqueness of each people group,(*ethne*). The glory, honor and splendor of the nations comes from the Lord and will be presented before Him in heaven (Revelation 21:24-26). The color, the texture, the fragrance, and the music of each culture is woven into the tapestry of God's awesome and diverse attributes which are distributed among the nations to reflect his majesty and glory.

How does a Christian artist respond to these four distinctives?

Through our music Colin Harbinson says:
1. We affirm the redeemable
2. We oppose the demonic
3. We reform the distorted
4. We celebrate the natural

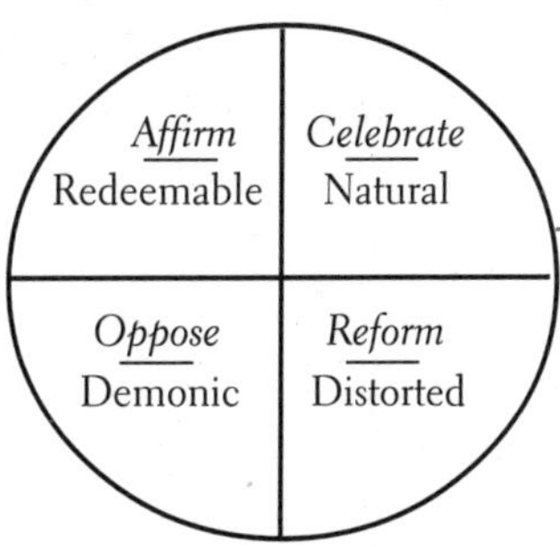

For example, a certain country in Asia treats women as second class citizens. This sexist distortion is so traditional that it is even found among professing Christians. Songs which reflect a biblical view of the honor due women will not only esteem the women of this particular nation, but aid in the discipling of this nation (Ephesians 5:25-33). Music can help reform a traditional distortion to a biblical precedent. Music and art can reinforce kingdom culture and values by affirming the redeemable aspects of cultures.

- Songs that proclaim justice and affirm decency bring salt and light among the nations (Amos 5:24).
- Worship that engages in spiritual warfare against the powers and principalities of darkness and opposes participation in demonic rituals and traditions (Psalm 149:6-9; Deuteronomy 18:9-13).
- Songs that deplore injustice, denounce the oppression of the poor and proclaim true liberty in Christ and combat distortions that keep the poor in an endless cycle of poverty (Amos 5:11-15).
- Music and art can help a culture celebrate the Lord and the uniqueness of His design for them as they come under His Kingdom rule and authority.

The Lausanne Covenant, created during the 1974 Lausanne Consultation on World Evangelization, states that in every culture the church must be allowed to indegenize itself, and to celebrate, sing and dance the Gospel in its own cultural medium while avoiding syncretism (association with evil elements) and provincialism (a retreat into their own culture which cuts them off from the church at large).

The church is a supra-ethnic community. Therefore, while rejoicing in our cultural inheritance and developing our own indigenous forms, we must always remember that our primary identity as Christians is not in our particular culture but in the one Lord and His one body (Ephesians 4:3-6).[5]

We are not called as artists to westernize the artistic expression of another culture's worship. We are called to speak God's truth into all nations and help them to express their obedient response through their own heart language. As popular as western music is throughout the world, we must resist the temptation of imposing our own styles on other cultures and concentrate on raising up new storytellers and artists within these cultures who understand and speak the "heart language" of their people group.

It is the storytellers who have passed down the distortions from generation to generation. The priests, the artists and the poets have echoed the deceptions throughout the ages.

It is the storytellers who have convinced Wugomi and his people that they will always be poor, so they have accepted this destiny for generations. It is the storytellers who have pronounced the death penalty on Naopli and thousands of other widows among the Yali people for centuries.

It is the storytellers who have condemned Mikko and millions of women to a life of servitude and matrimonial slavery as second class citizens. It is the storytellers who have convinced cultures to abandon the elderly, worship ancestors, sacrifice to idols, eat the flesh of men, abort the unwanted, eliminate the undesirable, and emaciate themselves to obtain cleansing and forgiveness.

We, as Christian artists and musicians are also storytellers. We come with a different story. Partnering with church planting movements, we come with His story and proclaim the good news of God's redemption and healing. We tell the story of truth and disciple the nations by singing the decrees which make for a wise and understanding nation (Deuteronomy 4:6), teaching them to obey all Christ has commanded (Matthew 28:19).

We help raise up a generation of new storytellers among the nations- not to build a Utopia here on earth, but to reflect God's glory and wisdom among all peoples!

Epilogue

It was the most beautiful instrument she had ever seen. The little girl pressed her nose against the frosted window of the music shop. There in the midst of shiny new trumpets with bright red Christmas bows lay a little violin just her size. Leaning against a beautifully gift wrapped box was the treasure which topped her Christmas list.

Oh, if Mom and Dad only knew how much she dreamed about that little violin and how she pictured herself playing the sweetest melodies.

But the little girl's parents had noticed how she stopped by the music shop window every day on the walk home from school. And they had secretly put a deposit down on the instrument.

When Christmas morning arrived the little girl bounded down the stairs to the cozy den where the decorated tree stood. All night long it seemed, she had wondered if her prayers would be answered.

And now the moment had arrived. Her sleepy eyes gazed over a myriad of green and red and silver boxes. Her little heart pounded as she looked for anything that resembled that special box in the window.

There! Yes there to the back of the tree was a box that could be...yes it looked just like the one in the window.

Mom and Dad both had that special grin on their faces and by now she knew her dream had come true. She headed straight to the box and pulled the ribbon undone. Lifting off the lid she almost closed her eyes as if to prolong the sheer excitement of the moment.

There was the brown leather case and in the soft scarlet velvet lining rested the most beautiful little violin in the world. "This is the bestest Christmas ever," she exclaimed as she wrapped her arms around mom and dad.

"Now, we have signed you up for lessons as soon as school starts back," her Mom said.

"Yes," Dad piped in, "With one of the greatest teachers in the entire city. A maestro who has taught some of the greatest violinists around."

"So, we are expecting you to work hard and learn everything you can about playing the violin," Mom said.

"And practice too," Dad added.

"Oh I will, I will," the little girl said with determination.

Dad was right. The maestro was a great master of the violin. The little girl sat in amazement as he showed her everything about the violin. And when he played, it was almost like a ballerina dancing smoothly and precisely over the strings. It was majestic! The little girls dreams of skillfully playing the sweetest melodies captured her every thought.

Oh, how wonderful it would be to please her teacher and honor him by learning everything he so lovingly taught her. But it was hard work. The maestro commanded deep commitment and an abiding faithfulness, and the little girl put everything she had into her practice.

Although she looked forward to each new lesson, she knew he would challenge her to greater heights. Lesson after lesson, and practice after practice, finally the squeaky sounds gave way to a steady note. Finally the fingers danced and the violin sang it's beautiful melody.

It was hard, but it was glorious.

But, of course, all of this was behind a closed door in her bedroom or at the maestro's studio.

The Spring recital was just around the corner and all the young students shared the nervous notion of going public. The little girl was no exception so she worked even harder. She knew her performance would reflect everything her master had taught her.

Everyday she spent special time reviewing his violin book. Going over each lesson and memorizing each principle, her confidence began to grow. It wasn't so much a confidence in herself but more a confidence in her master and his word.

"If you abide in this faithfully," he said, "you will play the violin and play it well."

The Spring recital arrived so quickly and all the young students dressed in their Sunday best, arrived at the downtown concert hall.

Moms, dads, aunts, uncles, and even the mayor began to take their seats in the auditorium. The place was packed and full of nervous expectations. The lights dimmed, the curtain opened, and one by one each student took their place at center stage. It was a wonderful evening and each violinist glimmered like a little star in the night sky.

The little girl was the last student to perform. She sat quietly behind the side curtain her mind busy at work, going over every note of the piece she would play. Every crescendo, and every portamento was so important because her teacher had taught her every step of the way. She wanted to present her work with passion back to the master of the song.

It was her turn. She stepped out on stage and into the light. A thousand faces stared back at her. Silently she lifted the little violin to her shoulder. With bow in position and chin up she closed her eyes and began to play.

The audience could not believe their ears. Although each of the students had played well, something special filled the air. Like a graceful ballerina, this little girl's song danced smoothly and precisely over the strings of her little violin. It was majestic!

All the while, with her eyes closed, she clearly focused on one thing–her master and all that he'd taught her. And with each sweep of the bow came the sweetest melody. Finally that last glorious note echoed into forever as she held her bow high in the air.

The audience stood to their feet and the applause grew louder than a hundred waves crashing onto shore. The mayor was exuberant, and Mom and Dad wept in that special pride only parents share.

But the little girl seemed not to notice at all. Her face was expressionless as her eyes peered out into the audience. Past the mayor, past her parents, past the cheering audience, she searched for the great master for whom she had played. Where was the maestro?

Finally, there on the front row of the balcony sat that man she had grown to love and respect with such devotion. There was the teacher who called for dedication, faithfulness, and practice. Still seated, his eyes looked straight into hers as if he were right in front of her and within reach. For the little girl it felt like forever as she waited for her master, the great maestro, to respond.

Suddenly, in one swift moment he stood triumphantly to his feet and yelled, "**Bravo!**"

And then a smile broke across the little girl's face.

"And then the Lord said, 'Well done good and faithful servant'" (Matthew 25:21).

ENDNOTES

CHAPTER ONE

1. *Concise Theology*, J.I. Packer, Tyndale House Publishers, Inc. (Wheaton, IL 1993) p. 80.
2. *Future Grace*, John Piper, Multnomah Books, (Sisters, OR 1995) p. 9.
3. *Letters of C.S. Lewis*, C.S. Lewis, Harcourt, Brace and World, Inc. (New York, NY 1966) p. 256.
4. *Future Grace*, John Piper, p. 94.
5. Ibid., p. 9.
6. Frank Zappa.
7. "Faces Rocks," Dec. 1986, p. 24.
8. *Plugged In*, Focus on the Family, Aug. 1996, p. 7.
9. *Future Grace*, John Piper, p. 87.
10. *Release*, May/June 1996.
11. *Roaring Lambs*, Rob Briner, Zondervan Publishing House (Grand Rapids, MI, 1993) p.29.
12. *Future Grace*, John Piper, p.212.
13. *The Great Divorce*, C.S. Lewis, Macmillan, (New York, NY 1946) p. 81.
14. *One Holy Passion*, lecture series R.C. Sproul, Ligonier Ministries.
15. *Future Grace*, John Piper, p. 9.
16. *Perspectives on the World Christian Movement*, Ralph Winter, William Carey Library, (Pasadena, CA 1982) p. 137.
17. *Future Grace*, John Piper, p. 9.
18. *Be Thou My Vision*, Text Ancient Irish Hymn translated by Mary E. Byrne, Versified by Eleanor H. Hull.

CHAPTER TWO

1. Quoted in Leighton Ford, *Transforming Leadership* InterVarsity Press (Downer's Grove, IL 1991) p. 37.
2. G.D. Watson, Good News Publishers.

CHAPTER THREE

1. Howard Hendricks (from a public sermon).
2. Attributed to Os Guiness.
3. Attributed to Shakespeare.
4. *CCM* Magazine, June 1996.
5. *Future Grace*, John Piper, p. 149.
6. Ibid., p. 224.
7. *Webster's Dictionary*.
8. *Chamber's 20th Century Dictionary*.
9. New American Standard Bible.
10. *Honesty, Morality and Conscience*, Jerry White, NavPress, (Colorado Springs, 1979) p. 78.

150

11. *Discipline of Grace*, Jerry Bridges, NavPress, (Colorado Springs, 1994) p. 143.
12. *Kingdom of Priests Study Guide*, Gerrit Gustafson Worship Seminar.
13. *Descending into Greatness*, Bill Hybels, Zondervan, (Grand Rapids, MI, 1995).
14. *Rebuilding Your Broken World*, Gordon MacDonald, Thomas Nelson Publishers, (Nashville, TN, 1988).
15. *Carry a Big Stick*, George Grant, Highland Books, (Elkton, MD, 1996).

CHAPTER FOUR

1. Gene Edward Veith, Jr. *The Gift of Art*, InterVarsity Press, (Downer Grove, IL 1983) p. 21.
2. Ibid., p. 22.
3. Ibid., p. 23.
4. Tony Evans, *Are Christians Destroying America?* Moody Press, (Chicago, IL 1996) p. 39.
5. The song "Spark" by Aleixa, Liquid Disc Records, Aleixa Album.
6. The song " 1 Could Murder" by Aleixa Disc Records, Aleixa Album.
7. The song "Scarified" by Klank, 1996 Spinning Audio Vortex Publishing. Klank-*Still Suffering* Album.
8. John Piper, *Desiring God*, Multnomah, (Portland, OR 1986) p. 66.
9. John Stott, from *Perspectives on the World Christian Movement*, William Carey Library, (Pasedena, CA) p. 3.
10. Harold Best, *Music Through the Eyes of Faith*, Harper SanFrancisco, (San Francisco, 1993), p. 171.

CHAPTER FIVE

1. Gene Edward Veith, Jr. *The Gift of Art*, IVP 1983, p. 25.
2. Dr. David K. Blomgren, *Song of the Lord*, Bible Press, (Portland, OR 1978) p. 26.
3. Ibid, p.26-27.
4. Ibid., p. 25.
5. Gene Edward Veith, Jr., *The Gift of Art*, IVP. 1983, p. 6.

CHAPTER SIX

1. Dr. David K. Blomgren, *Song of the Lord*, Bible Press, (Portland, OR 1978) p. 30.
2. George Sweeting, *Great Quotes & Illustrations*, Word Publishing, (Waco, TX 1985), p. 188.
3. Ibid., p. 188.
4. Gene Edward Veith, Jr. *The Gift of Art*, IVP. 1983, p. 36.
5. Focus on the Family, 1990, 1994, Chuck Colson Article from his books, *Who Speaks for God?* 1985 and *The God of Stones and Spiders*, 1990 (Crossway Books, Wheaton, IL).

6. Gene Edward Veith Jr. *The Gift of Art*, IVP 1983.
7. David Baroni "We Don't Worship the Worship," Integrity Music.

CHAPTER SEVEN

1. John Piper, *Let The Nations Be Glad*, Baker Book House, (Grand Rapids, 1993) p. 11.
2. Statistics from The U.S. Center for World Mission, Pasadena, CA.
3. Tom Avery, *Mission Frontiers* magazine, May-August 1996.
4. John Stott, "Making Christ Known," *Historic Documents from the Lausanne Movement*, Paternoster Press 1996, p. 105. (note #4 is listed #1 under *How Can Music Disciple The Nations*).
5. John Stott, "Making Christ Known," *Historic Documents from the Lausanne Movement*, Paternoster Press 1996, p. 102.

Appendix One
A Covenant for Ministry

Below is a sample of the wording of a covenant that you should consider to make a part of your music ministry. Prayerfully consider the wording of this agreement and sign it with reverence for this covenant is between you and God.

MINISTRY STANDARDS

I pledge before the Lord Jesus Christ to stand for Him in ministry through my music and/or artistic abilities on the foundation of the following ministry standards:

1. Personal Devotion

My personal and private growth in devotion to the Lord Jesus and His Word will always hold priority over the advancement of any public ministry or work.

2. Accountability

I reassert my commitment to the Lord through a commitment to local church ministry involvement and the voluntary participation in a small group of Christian peers with whom I will nurture openness in areas of personal devotion, purity, family, work, rest, and exercise.

"Whether I eat or drink or whatever I do, I do all for the glory of God" (1 Corinthians 10:31).

3. Proclamation

My ministry will always strive to promote the reputation and name of the Lord Jesus Christ over my own reputation; and the advancement of Christ's Kingdom over my own career. I will obey the biblical mandate of the Great Commission and be open to serving the Lord cross-culturally as He leads me.

4. Performance

My public performance will seek to glorify God and express that which is spiritually, morally and ethically pure.

5. Progress

I will regularly rededicate the development of my own artistic gift to the primary agenda of proclaiming Christ's gospel and the worship of the Lord God Almighty—whether or not I ever attain a music- or arts-related occupation.

6. Reproduction

I commit regularly and prayerfully to seek out other artists in Christian music ministry, even those who may one day surpass me in artistic ability and notoriety—whom I can mentor and train. That is, I will apply the general Christian principle of discipleship to the specific arena of intentionally seeking to reproduce other music/arts-oriented ministers, as I go about exercising my own artistic abilities in ministry.

"And the things you have heard me say in the presence of many witnesses entrust to reliable (people) who will also be qualified to teach others."

II Timothy 2:2 (NIV, clarification added)

____

signature

____

print your name

____

date

Adapted from Artists in Christian Testimony

Appendix Two

Resources for Ministry

Music and Missions Opportunities

1. Musician's Summer of Service
    Youth with a Mission
    P.O. Box 3000
    Lakeside, MT 59922
    (406) 844-2221   fax (406) 844-3730
    Short term summer missions trips for contemporary artists

2. Campus Crusade for Christ
    Keynote Communications
    13232 Old Meridian St.
    Carmel, IN 46032
    (317) 571-2077   fax (317) 571-2078
    e-mail: charlieberry@juno.com (Recruiting Dept.)

3. Artists in Christian Testimony
    Contact: Byron Spradlin
    P.O. Box 395
    Franklin, TN 37065-0395
    (615) 591-2598   fax (615) 591-2899
    email: 74152.727@compuserve.com
    Placing career artists on the mission field worldwide.

4. Celebrant Singers
    P.O. Box 1416
    Visalia, CA 93279
    Contact: Harlan Hutson
    (209) 627-4000   fax (209) 740-4040
    web site: www.celebrant.com
    Short term choral and instrumental touring groups.

5. Church Resource Ministries
    Contact: Steve Hoke
    1709 Coolcrest Ave.
    Upland, CA 91786
    (714) 779-0370
    e-mail: 74543.3221@compuserve.com
    Worship leaders training for local churches.

6. Frontiers
   325 N. Stapley Dr.
   Mesa, AZ 85203
   Contact: Grace Wiebe
   (602) 834-1500   fax (602) 834-1974
   e-mail: Grace.Wiebe@canada.telcom.lfa.com
   Ethnomusicologists assisting church planting teams in
   Muslim areas.

7. Greater Europe Mission "Project Proclaim"
   18950 Base Camp Road
   Monument, CO 80132
   (719) 488-8008   fax (719) 488-8018
   Web site: www.gemusa.org
   Professional jazz teams in Europe.

8. Operation Mobilization
   Contact: Frank Fortunato
   P.O. Box 444
   Tyrone, GA 32090
   (770) 631-0432   fax (770) 631-0432
   e-mail: fort@omusa.om.org
   Short term teams of classical, jazz, folk, praise bands, drama
   and mime teams. Music coordinators on OM ships.

9. Pioneers Field Ministries
   Contact: Dave Hall
   12343 Narcoossee Rd.
   Orlando, FL 32827
   (407) 382-6000   fax (407) 382-1008
   Worship musicians working with church planting teams among
   the unreached.

10. Musicians for Missions
    Youth With a Mission
    attn: Karen Lafferty
    P.O. Box 22009
    Sante Fe, NM 87502
    (505) 471-5872
    e-mail: 100340.3723@compuserve.com
    Short term contemporary bands, soloists, praise bands, drama
    and mime groups. Ethnic dance teams.

11. Summer Institute of Linguistics (SIL)
    Ethnomusicology Program
    Contact: Dr. Tom Avery
    7500 W. Camp Wisdom
    Dallas, TX 75236
    (972) 708-7400, ext.2265 fax (972) 708-7387
    e-mail: tom_Avery@sil.org.
    Trained ethnomusicologists assisting tribal groups in indigenous worship.

12. Music in World Cultures
    Crown College Graduate Studies
    Contact: Dr. John Benham
    6425 Court Rd. 30
    St. Bonifacius, MN 55375
    (800) 910-GRAD fax. (612) 446-4250
    e-mail: benhamj@gw.crown.edu
    Accredited, graduate level course work for musicians and missionaries providing cultural insight to worldview through music.

13. Prairie Bible Institute
    Ethnomusicology Program
    Contact Vernon Charter
    P.O. Box 4000
    Three Hills, AB TOM2NO Canada
    (800) 661-2425   fax (403) 443-5540
    e-mail:vernon.charter@pbi.ab.ca
    Advanced theological, academic, technological and field-based studies, leading to career ministries in ethnomusicology.

14. AD 2000 Movement
    Worship & Arts Network
    P.O. Box 444
    Tyrone, GA 30290
    (770) 631-0432   fax (770) 631-0439
    e-mail ad2000wa@usa.om.org
    A global fellowship of classical, contemporary and cross-cultural musicians and artists committed to bring all peoples to worship the one true God.

Christian Music Seminars, Workshops and Fellowships

1. Christian Artist's Seminar USA
   475 West 115th Ave. Suite 6
   Denver, CO 80234
   (800)755-7464　　fax (303) 457-0623

2. Babbie Mason Music Seminar
   1480-F Terrell Mill Rd.
   Marietta, GA 30067
   (770) 952-1443　　fax (770) 984-0344

3. Gospel Music Week and the Gospel Music Academy
   c/o The Gospel Music Association
   1205 Division St.
   Nashville, TN 37203
   (615) 242-0303　　fax (615) 254-9755

4. Maranatha Worship Seminars
   The Corinthian Group
   30230 Rancho Viejo Road
   San Juan Capistrano, CA 92675
   (714) 248-4000

5. LaMar Boschman Worship Seminars
   P.O. Box 130
   Bedford, TX 76095
   (817) 540-1826　　fax (817) 354-9608

6. The Worship Group
   Contact: Gerrit Gustafson
   P.O. Box 3774
   Brentwood, TN 37024
   (615) 371-5151
   e-mail: worshipgroup@aol.com
   equipping churches and worship teams.

7. The Crucible
   P.O. Box 22061
   Nashville TN 37202
   (615) 327-1200　　fax (615) 227-0233
   Discipleship classes and outreaches for artists and musicians.

8. The Nashville Christian Musicians Fellowship
    P.O. Box 395
    Franklin, TN 37065
    (615) 591-2598   fax (615) 591-2599
    Monthly fellowship and accountability meetings.

9. Surrogate Sisters
    P.O. Box 681567
    Franklin, TN 37068-1567
    (615) 370-4795
    Fellowship for wives of itinerant music ministries

10. Christian Music Connection (CMC)
    John Platillero
    Knoxville, TN
    (423) 588-3232
    Musical and spiritual support for local Christian artists.
    Thirteen chapters of CMC throughout the U.S.
    www.cmcnet.org

Christian Artists Associations (Worldwide)

1. C.A. Association Germany
    P.O. Box 25
    64847 Shaafheim
    Germany
     49.6073.87149   fax. 49.6073.8251

2. C.A. Association Latvia
    E. Veidenbauma 10
    LV 3400 Liepaja
    Latvia   ph. 371.8.23424231

3. C.A. Association Music & Media
    P.O. Box 81065
    3009 GB Rotterdam
    Holland
    31.010.4568688 fax. 31.010.4559022

4. C.A. Association Nepal
    Solon Karthak
    P.O. Box 3358 Katmandu
    Nepal
     977.1.522251   fax. 977.1.226820

5. C.A. Association Slovakia
    Sreznevskeho 2
    Bratislava
    Slovakia

6. C.A. Association South Africa
    P.O. Box 35583
    Menlo Park
    0102 Pretoria
    South Africa
     27.012.474.858 fax 27.12.475.501

7. Christian Classical Musicians
    Bjulevagen 53
    12241 Enskede
    Sweden
    46.8.6734804   fax. 46.8.6734802

8. Continential Ministries
    Postbox 81065
    3009 GB Rotterdam
    Holland
    31.010.4568688 fax 31.010.4559022

9. The European Christian Artists Seminar
    Postbox 81065
    3009GB Rotterdam
    Holland
    31-10-4568688   fax 31-10-4559022

10. South African Gospel Music Seminar
    Creative Music
    Contact: Billy Paulson
    P.O. Box 7881
    Newton Park 6055
    Port Elizabeth, South Africa
    27-41-351550   fax 27-41-313168

For Further Reading

Music, Worship, and the Art

1. *The Contemporary Christian Music Debate* by Steve Miller, Tyndale House Publishers.
2. *The Gift of Art* by Gene Edward Veith, Jr., Intervarsity Press.
3. *State of the Arts* by Gene Edward Veith, Jr., Crossway Books (Appears to be an update of *The Gift of Art*.)
4. *Song of the Lord*, Dr. David Blomgren, Bible Press, Portland, OR.
5. *Contemporary Worship Music* (A Biblical Defense) John M. Frame, Presbyterian & Reformed Publishing.
6. *The Responsibility of The Christian Musician*, Glen Kaiser, Cornerstone Press.
7. *Music Through the Eyes of Faith*, Harold Best, Harper SanFrancisco, 1993.

Music, Missions, and World Cultures

1. *Let the Nations Be Glad*, John Piper, Baker Book House.
2. *Run with the Vision*, Bob Sjogren, Bill & Amy Stearns, Bethany House Publishers.
3. *Music in Missions* (Discipling Through Music) T.W. Hunt, Broadman Press.

Inspirational Reading

1. *The Discipline of Grace*, Jerry Bridges, NavPress.
2. *Transforming Leadership*, Leighton Ford, InterVarsity Press.
3. *Future Grace*, John Piper, Multnomah Books.
4. *Descending Into Greatness*, Bill Hybels, Zondervan Publishing House.
5. *No Compromise: The Life Story of Keith Green*, Melody Green, Sparrow Press, 1989.
6. *The Parable of Joy*, Michael Card, Thomas Nelson Publishers, 1995.

Scott Wesley Brown is working on building a library of resources for Christian musicians such as books on songwriting, custom album recording, worship, and ministry development. To obtain a current order form, write to: P.O. Box 1111, Franklin, TN 37065, USA.

Phone/fax (615) 595-8180

I CARE Ministries

I CARE MINISTRIES, "International Christian Artists Reaching the Earth," was founded by Scott Wesley Brown in 1983 during his first trip behind the Iron Curtain. Scott discovered scores of Christian musicians who wanted to evangelize through music, yet who had no musical instruments. After leaving his own guitar in Eastern Europe, Scott appealed to other Christian artists such as Amy Grant, Steve Camp, Bruce Carroll, and Carman who rallied behind I CARE's vision of equipping musicians in third world and restricted access countries. Since then Scott has delivered hundreds of musical instruments to Christian musicians in Africa, Asia, Eastern Europe and more recently, Cuba. He has also taken several teams into these nations bringing encouragement through ministry training seminars.

In our spiritually and musically blessed nation, we are apt to take for granted the endless supply of musical instruments and equipment available to us as Christians. The case is not the same in many restricted access and developing countries. I CARE MINISTRIES (International Christian Artists Reaching the Earth) is dedicated to getting musical instruments into the hands of Christians in these countries so that they, too, may experience the blessing of worshiping with beautiful music.

In the spirit of giving, please check your closets and storage spaces for musical instruments and equipment that you are no longer using...that old violin from fifth grade orchestra, the saxophone or guitar that got six lessons worth of use....and consider giving a special gift that will be used to further the Gospel to the ends of the earth! Your donations may be counted as year-end tax deductions.

I CARE Ministries
Attn: Scott Wesley Brown
P.O. Box 1111
Franklin, TN 37065
phone/fax (615) 595-8180
e-mail: swbicare@aol.com
www.community-web.com/icare

Artists in Christian Testimony (A.C.T.)

The Mission

Artists in Christian Testimony (A.C.T.) is a mission board and sending agency for arts and worship-based ministries and missionaries committed to local and world evangelization.

Their mission it to help equip the Church—and especially its artists and leaders—to more fully embrace the arts in our worship of God and in the task of proclaiming—in Christ's name—His truth, beauty, glory and salvation to all peoples of the world.

The Vision

To provide worship, music and arts-oriented ministers, ministries and missionaries the organizational "home base," administrative structures and accounting systems they need to find release for the ministries God assigns them—whether they are full time, part time or volunteer.

To provide church, mission and ministry leaders the resources of worship and arts-based ministry personnel, presentations, consulting, materials and strategies that will assist their particular ministry agendas.

Consider associating your ministry with A.C.T.:

˘ if you need for your ministry some or all of the following: professional association; administrative, donor and accounting services; proper organizational and legal accountability; and if needed, non-profit legal status.

˘ if you hold a general commitment to world evangelization and Christian leadership training, along with your specific arts-based ministry focus.

˘ if you are committed to effecting biblically and culturally relevant ministry for Christ through music and the arts—whether in worship, evangelism, leadership training, church planting, church growth, and/or market place impact.

The Benefits of A.C.T.:

1. The freedom to pursue God's creative and unique ministry calling (whether related to evangelism, worship, Christian leadership development, church planting, church growth, or market place Christian ministry);

2. An administrative ministry headquarters that works in conjunction with your own current personal or ministry accountability structure. (If accepted, your current 'accountability structure' becomes a committee of A.C.T.'s Board.);

3. The association, networking, guidance and consultation with other experienced arts-oriented innovative ministers, within a context of understanding, affirmation, and practical support.

By associating your ministry with A.C.T. you join an international coalition of Christian arts ministers (vocational, bi-vocational and volunteer) where your creative calling from God—a calling to integrate creative music or arts ministry strategies in church, missions and/or market place ministry endeavors—is seen to be correct rather than something strange.

A.C.T. brings your ministry into a ministry family that validates your creative calling, helps you pursue that calling, and guides you on solid biblical footing, with solid administrative and legal structure.

A.C.T. is not a booking agency. But it does regularly link its associated staff and ministries (who do their individual scheduling) to churches, organizations and events in need of arts ministry and resources.

Consider supporting A.C.T:

˘ if you realize that to reach the cultures of this globe for Christ, a new breed of worship and arts-based ministers, church planters and missionaries . . . sensitive to the values and attitudes of the never-churched (the lost) and the unchurched (the wandering). . . must be affirmed.

˘ if you realize that worship- and arts-based ministers, church planters and missionaries are not often affirmed, empowered and deployed for ministry but should be.

ˇ if you realize the Church must intentionally empower the army of worship and arts-based ministers, church planters and missionaries already out there commissioned by God—those already worshipers and disciples themselves, committed to the Word of God, experienced in ministry—just waiting to be legitimized for ministry.

ˇ if you realize that in our world today—most people either have no Christian or church background, are marinated by the media in non-Christian and non-biblical values, find most Christian church services boring and irrelevant to their daily lives, or desire 'spirituality' and 'contact' with the spiritual dimension, value the arts. And, if you realize that many worship and arts-based ministers are endowed by God in specialized ways to communicate the Gospel to these 'never-churched' people, whether in our own culture or cross-culturally.

ˇ if you realize that most Christians do not yet see the need to financially support these creative Kingdom servants, but you do.

Artists in Christian Testimony
Rev. Byron Spradlin, President & Director
P.O. Box 395 ˇ Franklin, TN 37065-0395
Phone (615) 591-2598 ˇ Fax (615) 591-2599
E-mail: ActNashville@worldnet.att.net

Order Form

Postal orders:
Scott Wesley Brown, P.O. Box 1111, Franklin TN 37065

Telephone orders: (615) 595-8180

Please send *Keeping the Gospel in Gospel Music* **to:**

Name:____

Address:____

City:_____________________________ State:________

Zip:__________

Telephone: (_____) ______________

Book Price: $10.00 in U.S. dollars.

Sales Tax: Please add 8.5% sales tax for books shipped to a
Tennessee address.

Shipping: $3.00 for the first book and $2.00 for each additional
book to cover shipping and handling within US,
Canada, and Mexico. International orders add $7.00
for the first book and $3.00 for each additional book.
(Checks must be on a U.S. Bank.)

Quantity Discounts Available - Please call for information
(615) 595-8180